Praise for *Supervision and Evaluation for Learning and Growth*

"Educational leaders who want to make a difference in the quality of teaching and learning in today's classrooms will increase their professional repertoire by reading this important book. It is a valuable resource to be accessed in everyone's professional library!"

—Marie M. Adair, Executive Director, New Jersey ASCD

"The reader will find refreshing insights in this comprehensive look at major educational topics such as supervision, teacher evaluation, professional development, and modeling effective teaching. In a time period where opinions often dictate educational change, the authors have presented reliable information that will be useful for educational improvement."

—Dr. James Rosborg, President, Illinois Council of Professors in Education Administration, Director of Master's in Education, McKendree University

"This is the most practical book out there on the professional development of teachers and school administrators. It provides a step-by-step process, and is appropriate for all teachers and administrators regardless of their years of experience. You will find it worth your while to read this book!"

—Mark Spool, PhD, President, Management Development Solutions, West Chester, PA

"This text guides the reader on a journey of change from within, which occurs by enabling teachers to become effective leaders. It is an invaluable tool for building capacity within districts."

—Amy Robinson, EdD, English Language Arts Content Area Specialist, Illinois Center for School Improvement

"The research-based practices outlined in this book will allow principals, supervisors, and teachers to gain the skills necessary to help students succeed. I highly recommend this text."

—Dr. Kevin J. O'Mara, Superintendent, Argo Community High School, President, Illinois High School District Organization

"I recommend this book to all school administrators, future administrators, or anyone who aspires to provide leadership in an education setting—indeed, to any educator who wants to excel. The authors provide a comprehensive framework for effective supervision and professional development. They have applied their vast experience and unparalleled knowledge and wisdom to develop this comprehensive volume. This is a MUST READ for education leaders!"

—Thomas P. Jandris, PhD, Senior Vice President for Innovation, Concordia University Chicago

"As great schools strive to continuously improve, resources such as this book are invaluable for educational leaders as they oversee professional development. The authors have done an excellent job creating a format that is user friendly, clearly outlining chapter objectives for the reader. The importance of effective supervision has never been more vital to evaluating instruction. I highly recommend using this book as a guide for leaders to better understand that process and promote high achievement for all learners."

—Michael Glover, Principal, McHenry Middle School, McHenry, Illinois

"As a staff developer, I appreciate the authors' approach to the ongoing nature of effective staff development. Included in their staff development model are research-based outcomes for a teacher formative and summative evaluation process that goes far beyond traditional 'one and done' professional development models."

—D. William Dodds, EdD, Executive Director, IL ASCD

"The authors have clearly articulated what is necessary to become an impactful educator and how leaders in education can guide that process. This book is an exceptional resource for education leaders who aspire to excel!"

—Alan Meyer, PhD, Executive Vice President, Concordia University Chicago

"The school leader is a critical piece in the success of student achievement as the authors have indicated. This book would be a good 'field' handbook for emerging, novice, and experienced administrators."

—F. Jane Cobia, EdD, Director Doctoral Program and Associate Professor, Orlean Bullard Beason School of Education, Samford University, Birmingham, AL

"The authors provide an excellent foundational manual for new and aspiring administrators as well as district personnel assigned the task of creating a well-integrated professional development plan. No longer can we afford to use the 'one size fits all' model when supervising and mentoring teachers. This is a must read for educators determined to make a positive impact on student outcomes by retooling instructional practices."

—Dr. Theresa Alberico-Madl, Superintendent, East Prairie School District 73, Skokie, IL

"I found the book was profound in that it really anchored my thinking and had direct application to many conversations in which I was engaged, both personally and professionally. It resonates with both my studies in leadership and my personal experiences in the classroom and as a school and district leader."

—Patrick Keeley, Principal, Almond Campus, Warren Township High School District 121, Gurnie, IL

"I would recommend this book to any school leader, or aspiring school leader, who is serious about leveraging the natural relationships between supervision, evaluation, and professional growth to promote continuous improvement in their learning environment. The authors have found a way to bring the essential elements of best practice together in a way that is sure to turn on more than a few proverbial lightbulbs. A practical read that will spend more time in your hands than on a shelf."

—Dr. Victor Simon III, Superintendent of Schools, Gower Elementary School District 62, Willowbrook and Burr Ridge, IL

"Within this timely and well-written book, you will find the key to systematically leading meaningful professional development in our schools—what could be more important for our teachers and their students?"

—Carol J Reiseck, EdD, Assistant Dean, Learning Technology and Innovation, College of Graduate and Innovative Programs, Concordia University Chicago

"Readers will find this book a valuable resource to reference as they are confronted with various challenges during their years of leadership. It will also serve all leaders well to make space on their professional library shelf for this well-documented leadership resource!"

—Dr. John F. Cindric, Jr., Professor of Leadership and Emotional Intelligence, The University of Findlay

"Anyone involved in the development of teachers will treasure this book. It provides a clear and focused approach to helping teachers become more reflective and effective as practitioners. This book will alter what you know and can do to better empower and grow teachers within a professional learning community. A must read for experienced and aspiring school leaders!"

—Paul Enderle, Superintendent of Schools, Oak Lawn-Hometown School, District 123, Oak Lawn, IL

"*Supervision and Improvement of Learning* will help educational leaders improve teaching and learning in their schools. The authors present a well-differentiated model for understanding the best ways to support each individual teacher's ongoing professional development. Great teaching is a combination of both skill and professional knowledge, which presents leaders with the unique challenge to develop all teachers from novice to savvy veteran. This book will explain the best practices to help every teacher grow from where they are to great teachers."

—Dr. Kevin Brandon, Dean of College of Education, Concordia University Chicago

"In an era of high accountability, this book provides practitioners with practical strategies for ensuring that all children have an effective teacher in their classroom. The exercises and discussion segments are both relevant and thought provoking for any school embarking on the journey of improving professional practice through meaningful evaluation and data analysis."

—Lynette Zimmer, EdD, Superintendent, Lake Villa School District 41, Illinois

Supervision and Evaluation for Learning and Growth

OTHER BOOKS BY THE AUTHORS

Action Research for Educators

Action Research for Educators, Second Edition

Challenging Students to Learn: How to Use Effective Leadership and Motivation Tactics

Discipline by Negotiation: Methods for Managing Student Behavior

How to Finish and Defend Your Dissertation: Strategies to Complete the Professional Practice Doctorate

Leading School Change: Maximizing Resources for School Improvement

Managing Human Resources and Collective Bargaining

Resource Management for School Administrators: Optimizing Fiscal, Facility, and Human Resources

Grant Writing: Practical Strategies for Scholars and Professionals

The Teacher Leader: Core Competencies and Strategies for Effective Leadership

Understanding Technology for Non-Technical Educators

Ethics and Politics in School Leadership: Finding Common Ground

Supervision and Evaluation for Learning and Growth

Strategies for Teacher and School Leader Improvement

Daniel R. Tomal, Robert K. Wilhite, Barbara J. Phillips, Paul A. Sims, and Nancy P. Gibson

ROWMAN & LITTLEFIELD PUBLISHERS, INC.
Lanham • Boulder • New York • London

Published by Rowman & Littlefield
A wholly owned subsidiary of The Rowman & Littlefield Publishing Group, Inc.
4501 Forbes Boulevard, Suite 200, Lanham, Maryland 20706
www.rowman.com

Unit A, Whitacre Mews, 26-34 Stannery Street, London SE11 4AB

British Library Cataloguing in Publication Information Available

Library of Congress Cataloging-in-Publication Data

ISBN 978-1-4758-1372-2 (hardcover)
ISBN 978-1-4758-1373-9 (paperback)
ISBN 978-1-4758-1374-6 (e-book)

Contents

Acknowledgments

Collectively, the authors of this book have served in public, private, and independent schools and organizations for over 200 years. In the smallest rural settings, in the largest housing projects, and in suburban communities of every size, we have been supported by supervisors and evaluators who have influenced our thinking about what professional learning and growth fosters and requires. We appreciate the groundbreakers and colleagues who have encouraged us to lead. They have mentored us to build the capacity of each teacher and every member of our staff. We are stronger and more resilient when we work together toward a goal.

We extend our appreciation to the thousands of students with whom we have worked at the infant, preschool, elementary, middle, high school, undergraduate, graduate, and adult levels. You remind us that teacher professional learning and growth must be continuous so we can prepare you for a world not yet fully imagined by us, but which requires you to acquire new information, skills, and multiple approaches to complex problems. We hope we have modeled all of these as we have guided you in a supportive, caring manner.

We thank those who have read our drafts and offered endorsements. Your suggestions and affirmations invigorated our efforts. Finally, we embrace our family and friends who have supported our efforts to make this book a reality. Your words of encouragement sustained us as we completed this work.

Foreword

Historically, when the supervising administrator announces a professional development day, there is a wailing and gnashing of teeth of biblical proportions with a rolling of eyes, a shrug of the shoulders, and utterances among the staff of "Here we go again—another day wasted away from our kids, and what kind of an expensive 'insultant' are they bringing in this time?"

It is frustrating in that professional development has generally been at the end of the list of things administrators have to do. Most professional development days are poorly planned; the focus of the training is usually of the newest fad or dictated from someone who knows very little about the problems and concerns of site-based administrators and what teachers desperately need for success with their students.

This new book from Tomal, Wilhite, Phillips, Sims, and Gibson will eliminate that frustration. It is a "game changer" that provides a detailed planning model for supervisors in their role to improve learning through authentic professional learning and growth for teachers. As opposed to the traditional in-service model of one size fits all, the writers provide differentiation in professional learning and growth in the same way that teachers are asked to differentiate for their students.

Instead of glittering generalities concerning teacher evaluation and integration of curriculum and instruction, a "road map" of specific strategies is provided for the supervisor and the classroom teacher to improve teacher and student performance. In the culture of educational hype and "quick-fix solutions" to teaching and learning, this book is unique in that it is research based on the best instructional and supervisory practices as well as on the many years of hands-on experience of the co-authors. It will become your "go-to" guide.

Dr. T. Roger Taylor, President, Curriculum Design for Excellence, Inc.

Introduction

Supervision, evaluation, and professional learning and growth of teachers should be linked to improve student performance. Together, they are among the most important responsibilities of twenty-first-century school leaders. This book has been written to incorporate an examination and analyses of theories and practices related to improvement of teacher quality and student learning.

The authors have witnessed and facilitated professional learning and growth of teachers at many levels over sustained time periods. The models and strategies described in this book have been found to be successful in guiding professional learning and growth of teachers at the classroom, grade, department, school, and district levels.

The educational system is at a juncture in which curricular, instructional, and assessment shifts are occurring in tandem for both students and teachers. In contrast to the 1970s, 1980s, and 1990s, when curricular objectives, instructional models, and assessment processes were each given a successive decade of individual focus, schools are experiencing rapid changes in all these areas at the same time. These changes highlight the direct link between student and teacher instruction and learning.

The ratification of the *Common Core State Standards* (CCSS) in 2010 by the majority of the chief state school officers across the nation set a high bar of expectations upon which curriculum is to be developed or adjusted. *Race to the Top* (RTTT) offered 4.35 billion dollars in grants to states willing to address a number of areas that included the development of policies requiring the use of new, rigorous standards for students; the identification of planned efforts to improve teaching; the adoption of more helpful ways to measure teacher effectiveness; and the building of monitoring systems to track student growth.

Many states are requiring more rigorous superintendent, principal, and teacher preparation programs and licensure requirements. Calls for more effective systems to evaluate teachers include the advocating of a shift from the traditional evaluation process of conducting a few classroom observations and a written narrative that is "filed away" to meet legal requirements to a more effective, ongoing process of learning and growth during the year that is interactive as well as collegial and collaborative in nature.

This growth-oriented process of feedback, based on evidence drawn from visits to the classroom, is the focus of the relationship between school leader and teacher, which contributes to the development of an individual plan of learning and practice for each teacher. As a consequence, it is important for teachers and evaluators to have an understanding of the interrelatedness of supervision, evaluation, and professional learning and growth.

Moreover, there continues to be a need for both administrators and teachers to share a common language and knowledge of effective teaching models and their relationship to national and state standards. Likewise, there is a continued need for all educators to understand the importance of differentiated professional learning and growth for both nontenured and tenured teachers who are effective and who are struggling.

Although this book is primarily directed toward public schools, the strategies in this book can be effective for independent, private pre-K through 12 schools, and charter schools. The principles and strategies are practical and useful for any school educator or graduate student preparing to lead school improvement efforts and professional learning and growth.

Chapter 1 defines and brings specificity to the terms *supervision, evaluation,* and *professional learning and growth.* The history of supervision and evaluation processes and emergence of professional learning and growth are examined. The significant roles of values, mission, and vision are emphasized. A case study, thoughtful exercises, and discussion questions set the context for supervision and professional learning and growth.

The second chapter examines models and standards for effective teaching. State professional teaching standards, national boards for professional teaching standards, and research on effective teaching and its relationship to student achievement are elucidated. Various teaching frameworks, including alignment between models and standards, are also presented. Application is invited through presentation of a case study. A new teacher evaluation system is being developed in a district, and the reader is elected to be a representative on that district team. The reader has the opportunity to apply the principles in the chapter in a realistic school setting.

The third chapter examines the research on teacher effectiveness. The elements of the professional learning and growth plan are highlighted. The roles undertaken by the school leader during supervision and evaluation are illuminated. Consideration is given to the needs of both novice and veteran teachers with practical examples. At the close of this chapter, the reader is challenged to contribute to the development of two professional learning and growth plans, applying one's growing understanding of the elements that should be included in an effective plan.

The fourth chapter illustrates a professional learning and growth model of supervision and evaluation that incorporates a cycle of ongoing observations with professional dialogue and feedback based on evidence. The importance of responsive, constructive feedback during the supervisory phase is explained and illustrated. The role of the school leader in developing the individual professional learning and growth plan with the teacher and the school culture, which fosters the implementation and monitoring of the plan, are highlighted. This chapter concludes with a case study and discussion questions.

Chapter 5 describes how to actually implement a professional learning and growth model. The "loose-tight coupling leadership theory" is illustrated, which requires both assertive leadership and flexibility in how the school and teachers achieve goals that are prioritized. The school leaders' roles as supervisors and evaluators are examined. The relationship of formal requirements and informal, supportive interactions is emphasized. Exercises and a case study are included.

Chapter 6 focuses on teacher evaluation. Several state mandates and teacher evaluation approaches are presented. The topic of goal setting and how to conduct teacher evaluations are given detailed, step-by-step coverage. In addition, coaching, remediation, and developing performance improvement plans are discussed. The chapter concludes with a comprehensive review and examples of state and federal laws affecting teacher evaluations. Like the other chapters, a case study, along with exercises and discussion questions, is provided to give the reader an opportunity to apply the information.

In closing, chapter 7 invites the reader to follow the journey of one middle school in developing a professional learning and growth plan at the school level. It illustrates the relationship between the school plan and the district plan; it shows the relationship between the school plan and the individual plan. Finally, it emphasizes how the three levels can move together, in one direction, to achieve the stated goals. The chapter traces an eight-step process with examples at each stage of the journey.

The process begins with an examination of the values, mission, and vision of the district. Data collection and analyses are emphasized as school leaders uncover the needs of teachers and build their capacities as individuals and as a group. After a plan is developed, with checkpoints for monitoring, implementation occurs. Adjustments are made along the way. At the end, the accomplishments are celebrated, and reflections are noted for use in future school improvement efforts.

The final chapter is practical and illustrative, and shows the direct linkage between and among district-wide, school-wide, and individual teacher learning and growth planning. It invites the reader to integrate how professional learning and growth can be undertaken through illustration and application in a case study that concludes the chapter.

FEATURES OF THE BOOK

This book is succinctly written and an insightful read for graduate students and practicing educators. This book is unique in that it provides many engaging examples that can be used by all. One feature of the book is the correlation of each chapter's objectives with professional organizational standards of the *Interstate Teacher Assessment and Support Consortium*, (InTASC), the *Interstate School Leaders Licensure Consortium* (ISLLC), the *Educational Leadership Constituent Council* (ELCC), the *Teacher Leader Model Standards*, and the *Learning Forward Standards*.

Another valuable feature of the book is the incorporation of many leadership strategies, teacher evaluation and instructional improvement processes, data and research, school improvement models, resources, and teacher evaluation techniques. The information is presented in a clear-cut and practical manner. The topics in this book are useful for any school educator who desires to learn principles and strategies for initiating and evaluating school improvement and improving student performance.

Other features of this book include:

- the rationale for the shift away from traditional teacher evaluation models
- the value of the new professional learning and growth models
- practical examples of what the shift involves
- strategies for supervising and evaluating teachers
- illustrations of ongoing, embedded professional learning
- a comprehensive description of resources needed for school supervision
- examples of conducting teacher assessments
- a review of national, state, and district policies and laws
- strategies in evaluating teacher effectiveness

ORGANIZATION OF THE BOOK

The organization of this book has been designed so educators can understand principles, models, and strategies of leading school supervision and improvement of learning. Each chapter builds upon the other. However, each chapter is also distinct in itself, because it illustrates a specific topic as part of the development of a culture of professional learning and growth. Lastly, each chapter includes basic theories and examples of applying these theories, case studies, and exercises and discussion.

1

✛

Defining Supervision, Evaluation, and Professional Learning

OBJECTIVES

At the conclusion of this chapter you will be able to:

1. Review the historical context of supervision, evaluation, and professional development (ELCC 1, 2, 4, 6; ISLLC 1, 2, 3, 4, 6; InTASC 1, 2, 3, 4, 5, 6, 7, 8, 9, 10; Learning Forward Standards).
2. Distinguish between the concepts of supervision, evaluation, and professional learning (ELCC 1, 2, 5, 6; ISLLC 1, 2, 3, 5, 6; TLEC 1, 2, 3, 4, 5; InTASC 1, 2, 3, 4, 5, 6, 7, 8, 9, 10; Learning Forward Standards).
3. Understand the relationships between supervision, evaluation, and professional learning in a Professional Learning and Growth Model (ELCC 1, 2, 5, 6; ISLLC 1, 2; TLEC 1, 2, 3, 4, 5; InTASC 1, 2, 3, 4, 5, 6, 7, 8, 9, 10; Learning Forward Standards).
4. Design a Professional Learning and Growth Model for all teachers in a school (ELCC 1, 2, 3, 5, 6; ISLLC 1, 2, 3, 5, 6; TLEC 1, 2, 3, 4, 5; InTASC 1, 2, 3, 4, 5, 6, 7, 8, 9, 10; Learning Forward Standards).
5. Determine the best Professional Learning and Growth Model to meet the needs of all teachers (ELCC 1, 2, 3, 5; ISLLC 1, 2, 3, 5, 6; TLEC 1, 2, 3, 4, 5; InTASC 1, 2, 3, 4, 5, 6, 7, 8, 9, 10; Learning Forward Standards).

A HISTORY OF SUPERVISION AND EVALUATION

As America became a country in the 1770s, schools emerged as one part of the new democracy. In the communities they served, teachers were seen as key shapers of this democracy. To watch over teachers and ensure that they followed community norms and values, clergy and distinguished citizens became *supervisors*, who emphasized *strict control* and *close inspection* of school facilities and operations. These community supervisors evaluated teacher performance, monitored instruction, reviewed materials, and approved curriculum.

In the 1800s, specialized roles began to emerge. This was due to the increase in the number of schools. The person in charge of the administrative duties became known as the *principal teacher*. This leader or supervisor was in charge of everything from building maintenance to school materials and day-to-day teaching. A key figure, Horace Mann, emerged as a powerful voice for common public education.

Arguing that universal public education was the best way to turn the new nation's children into disciplined citizens, Mann gained widespread approval from those attempting to establish a public system of schooling across America. Most states adopted one version or another of the system he established in Massachusetts, especially the program for normal schools to train professional teachers. Educational historians credited Mann as the "Father of the common school movement."

During the rise of the Industrial Revolution in the 1900s, Frederick Taylor fostered the *efficiency movement* that led to mid-level managers who used supervision to *rate worker effectiveness*. A mechanical engineer, he sought to standardize industrial efficiency. He was one of the highly intellectual leaders in the Progressive Era of the 1900s. Taylor summed up his efficiency techniques in his book *The Principles of Scientific Management*. This movement carried over to education as school supervisors began to use the same type of checklists to rate teacher effectiveness within the classroom.

In the middle 1900s, John Dewey focused on autonomy, freedom, and democracy. Supervision involved inviting teachers to *reflect and experiment*. He was a major voice of progressive education. This progressive view contributed to the conflict between the role of supervisor as *teacher evaluator* and *helpful colleague*. This idea was further expanded as education moved through the late 1940s and 1950s.

In the 1950s, the list of duties of supervisors included *classroom visitation and observational practices*, but building management was the prime responsibility for most school leaders. Also, during this time, supervisors focused on teacher evaluation systems that would *monitor* teachers for *compliance* and would punish those who did not conform.

Clinical supervision was the primary focus of supervisors in the 1960s and 1970s. The supervisor was envisioned as a *colleague versus an evaluator*. Five phases of clinical supervision included the pre-observation conference, the classroom observation, the analysis of the observation, the post-observation conference, and the shared review of the analysis. The use of clinical supervision became a standard practice still used to this day.

In the 1980s, Madeline Hunter created her *seven-step model of lesson design*, which became a teacher rating checklist in many school districts. The Hunter Model of lesson design included the following elements: the anticipatory set, the objective and purpose, the input, the modeling, the checking for understanding, the guided practice, and the independent practice.

In the mid-1980s, two other approaches to supervision emerged. *Differentiated supervision* was a model that gave teachers choices, based on their experience and expertise, in their approaches to instruction. For new teachers, there was a need for intensive development and improvement to learn the art and craft of teaching. For experienced teachers, cooperative development became the best choice. Outstanding teachers used self-directed development.

In *developmental supervision*, the right approach to supervision for teachers depended upon their experience and expertise as well. For problematic teachers, direct control was needed. Inexperienced teachers required directive informational supervision. Veteran teachers were best served by collaborative or non-directive supervision.

In the early 1980s teacher evaluation was critically reviewed. An important study by the RAND Corporation written by Wise et al. (1984) found four consistent problems with supervision and evaluation. Each of these problems highlighted the need for reform in these areas. Figure 1.1 provides a brief summary of these obstacles in supervision and evaluation.

1. School leaders may lack the resolve and competency.

2. Teachers may resist because they lack a clear understanding of the processes involved.

3. There may be a lack of uniform practices within the school or district.

4. There may be a lack of training for supervisors, evaluators and teachers.

Figure 1.1. Obstacles to Effective Supervision and Evaluation

One example of reform in supervision and evaluation was the work of Charlotte Danielson (2007). Her *Framework for Teaching* became a popular model of supervision and evaluation in school districts. Her framework describes the full complexity of teaching. A key strength of the Danielson model is that it provides a common language for professional conversations.

Further reform in supervision and evaluation also came from two federal initiatives. The *No Child Left Behind Act* (NCLB, 2001) and the *Race to the Top* (2011) added accountability measures to school districts, school leaders, and teachers. More about these federal initiatives will be found in chapter 2. Throughout the history of supervision and evaluation, there have been various conflicting perspectives and insights into what is good teaching and learning. Table 1.1 highlights some of the key people and the approaches to supervision and evaluation.

Table 1.1. History of Supervision, Evaluation, and Professional Learning

Years	Movement	Advocates	Major Themes
1770–1900	Common school Universal schooling	Clergy Distinguished citizens Horace Mann	Inspection and oversight
1900–1945	Scientific progressive	Frederick Taylor John Dewey	Social efficiency Rating systems
1945–1975	Behavioral science Pragmatism	Abraham Maslow William Melchior Robert Goldhammer Morris Cogan	Learning theories Self-actualization Clinical supervision
1975–1990	Situational contingency	Madeline Hunter William Glatthorn Carl Glickman Charlotte Danielson	Seven-step model Differentiated supervision Developmental supervision Framework for supervision
2000–	Accountability and standards	Federal laws No Child Left Behind Race to the Top Standards alignment	Compliance testing Professional practice, evidence, and outcomes

DEFINING SUPERVISION

Every teacher knows the word *supervision*. This term is usually partnered with the word *evaluation*. Supervision and evaluation should be part of a continuum that leads to a third concept, *professional learning*. The experience of these three processes for a teacher is what constitutes a *Professional Learning and Growth Model*. Deeper explanations of these terms will be addressed in subsequent chapters.

Supervision can be broadly defined as the facilitation of what teachers and students do in the teaching and learning programs of schools. Supervisors are perceived as the monitors of the activities and the people in the school. The effective supervisor tries to ensure *good stewardship* of the time, talents, and assets of each person within the school community.

Supervision involves those activities that school leaders perform as *supervisors* in building relationships with teachers. Supervision enhances teacher instructional pedagogy, which should result in *increased student achievement*. Supervision involves many different people in the school community working together for the good of the students.

School leaders can be informal or formal leaders. An *informal school leader* can be a veteran teacher, a trusted colleague, or anyone else who helps a fellow teacher improve teaching and learning. A *formal leader* can be the principal, an assistant principal, a department head, a mentor, an academic coach, a grade-level leader, a teacher leader, or anyone else who has the role and function to help teachers improve their teaching and learning. Often, these formal leaders are called supervisors.

On some occasions, supervision is providing a teacher guidance or added support in how to teach a particular concept in a specified content area. Other times, supervision may involve affirming a teacher for teaching a lesson in which all students were engaged. A daily walk or *management by walking around* (MBWA) by the supervisor throughout all areas of the school gives the leader an overview and an ongoing assessment of how each person and program in the school is functioning.

Supervision is forming a relationship with all the teachers, staff members, students, parents, and members of the local community. The relationship with teachers is what most people think of when they hear the term *supervision*. This relationship extends over time and has the simultaneous purpose of enhancing the professional functioning of the teacher and monitoring the quality of those professional services.

Marzano, Waters, and McNulty (2005) developed a list of twenty-one responsibilities and associated practices of leaders that provide specific dimensions of supervision and evaluation of teachers. Of those twenty-one responsibilities, the top ten will be highlighted because they make the most difference in the lives of teachers and can increase student achievement.

- *Visibility*: Supervisors need to be present to teachers before, during, and after school so that teachers know the supervisors are there to help.
- *Involvement in the curriculum, instruction, and assessment*: Supervisors work with teachers to design effective units of instruction that incorporate key content, skills, best practices, and assessments.
- *Knowledge of the curriculum, instruction, and assessment*: Supervisors provide a deeper understanding of curriculum, instruction, and assessment by attending workshops, taking classes, and reading new books and articles. This knowledge is shared with teachers.
- *Affirming*: Supervisors celebrate with teachers their successes and help them deal with their failures and frustrations.
- *Resources*: Supervisors will do everything possible to provide teachers with the supplies, materials, or technology they need to make them successful in their classes.
- *Culture*: Supervisors build a vision of what the school can be and invite teachers to be a part of this ongoing vision.
- *Intellectual stimulation*: Supervisors engage teachers in continual dialogues on theories and best practices of teaching and learning.
- *Relationships*: Supervisors build professional relationships with teachers and invite them to become part of a professional learning community (PLC).
- *Communication*: Supervisors build open lines of communication so that every teacher feels connected. Communication is the lifeblood of the school community.
- *Monitoring and evaluating*: Supervisors assess and make formative evaluations about teachers constantly. This ongoing process leads to a summative evaluation that determines the teacher's status as a professional.

Each of the listed responsibilities describes the multifaceted picture of what supervision can be in the day-to-day experience of supervisors. In particular, supervisors continue to encourage, inspire, challenge, and motivate teachers to remain faithful to the mission of improving teaching and learning with the desired outcome of increased student achievement.

A clear example of effective supervision might include an *induction program* for a week or a few days that orientates new teachers to the culture and expectations of the school community. Supervisors empower new teachers by providing them with all the resources they need for teaching that can be found in the school. New teachers are also introduced to the staff members who can help the new teachers become successful.

New teachers are also introduced to *mentors* in an induction program. These mentors are experienced teachers who supervise and guide new teachers in lesson planning, classroom management, and other areas as they emerge. Mentors and mentees form a professional relationship in which the mentor frequently observes and confers with the mentee on how the teaching and learning is going.

Clinical supervision is another example of mentoring. In this one-on-one experience, the supervisor meets first with the teacher in a pre-observation conference to determine the areas of strength and areas in need of improvement on which to focus. The supervisor observes the teacher and looks at the focused areas in need of attention so that he or she can give directed and meaningful feedback to the teacher.

After the observation, the supervisor does an analysis on what was observed in the classroom and in the post-observation conference shares this analysis with the teacher. The conversation can lead to improvement of teaching and learning. After this, the two decide on how this one-on-one experience can further be improved. A more detailed explanation of clinical supervision will be provided in chapter 4.

Although clinical supervision is conducted by a principal or assistant principal and is a form of mentoring, it is also a clear example of *coaching*. In many schools today, there are literary and mathematics coaches who work one-on-one with teachers to observe, diagnose, and offer suggestions for improvements in teaching and learning. Coaching is another form of supervision because the focus is on helping teachers to be successful so that student learning increases.

Daily or weekly *walk-throughs* by the school leaders are another example of supervision. These observations have three purposes. First, the visits provide support for the teachers in letting them know that the school leader is interested in the teachers providing excellent teaching. Second, the visits inform the school leaders of the progress of teaching and learning in the school. And, third, the visits provide an opportunity for the students to see that the school leaders are supporting them in the learning process.

Feedback from supervisors on the walk-throughs is imperative for supervision. This directed and meaningful feedback helps teachers to grow by accepting their strengths. The feedback also helps teachers to address areas of needed improvement and leads to professional learning opportunities and experiences. Teachers want to hear praise and criticism about how they are doing. A quick e-mail, a short note, or a follow-up conversation are examples of the supervisor providing feedback.

Supervisors are often involved in the personnel issues of teachers. When there is a vacancy in teaching, the supervisor works with the district human resources personnel and a committee of teachers to interview and offer recommendations for the hiring of new teachers. The process becomes a collaboration guided by the supervisor setting a climate for peer sharing and building relationships.

Supervisors also monitor the daily attendance of teachers. The purpose of this is to make sure that every classroom has a qualified teacher present each day. When teachers are going to be absent, they normally talk to their supervisor and give the reason and date for the absence. The duty of the supervisor is to find a qualified substitute for these teachers.

Supervisors deal with the conflicts that arise between teachers. Sometimes teachers don't get along. There may be personality conflicts, jealousies, or a lack of understanding that causes conflicts. The duty of the supervisor is to bring teachers together to resolve these issues.

Supervisors also address areas of supervision that do not involve teachers. The supervisor needs to meet daily with the building maintenance supervisor to ensure that everything is working properly. Sometimes there are problems with a leaky roof, a faulty boiler, and a lack of electricity or water. All of these problems can interfere with the teaching and learning process. A supervisor has to be flexible and make adjustments when these things happen.

A pressing issue of schools today is the availability and use of technology. Supervisors need to meet often with the technology personnel to deal with such issues as appropriate use of the Internet, purchase of new equipment, and ongoing maintenance. Technology is a very important learning tool. Schools need to be prepared to meet the needs of teachers and students.

Another area that supervisors get involved with is in the transportation system of the school. Many schools use busing. Supervisors need to be attentive to the timing of student arrivals and dismissals. Special schedules have to be considered as do extracurricular events and after-school activities. Sometimes, there are student behavioral issues on the buses. A school supervisor must address these issues.

Weather is also something that supervisors need to have on their agenda. Inclement weather may prohibit the opening of school or force an early dismissal. Natural disasters such as hurricanes, tornadoes, or flash floods can interrupt schooling. Practice drills must become a part of the school routine to prepare teachers, students, and staff for these possibilities.

School safety is of paramount concern. With the increase in school violence, supervisors must safeguard students, faculty, and staff from dangerous elements and persons within or outside of the school. Locked doors, school identification cards, and other security measures must be taken into consideration.

Supervision involves leading all members of the school community in creating, implementing, and evaluating the key school *performance indicators* of *values, mission, vision, goals,* and *strategies.* The core values are the attitudes and behaviors that the school community believes are important. The mission states "who we are and why we exist." The vision points to what "we want to become." The goals are the school targets. The key strategies are the specific actions taken to achieve defined goals. Figure 1.2 gives examples of school performance indicators in an effective school.

Core Values	Respect, diversity, creativity.
Mission	Every child, every day success.
Vision	Learners today. Leaders tomorrow.
Goals	Increased literacy and numeracy in all grades.
Key Strategies	Engagement, groups, facilitation, coaching.
Key Indicators	Student writing and student performance that demonstrates use of multiplication to a math problem.

Figure 1.2.   Examples of Key Performance Indicators for an Effective School

Supervisors are like the conductor of an orchestra, bringing all parts of the orchestra together to ensure the smooth functioning of the musicians and to produce an outcome of quality music. In the case of schools, the outcome is increased teacher and student learning within a climate of trust and safety. The key school performance indicators all work together to create an environment in which teachers, students, school leaders, parents, and the local community work toward common goals and purposes.

Although these common purposes for the school ensure that all members are moving in the same direction, there also needs to be a focused direction for the approach to supervision in the school. Figure 1.3 provides examples of these school performance indicators for effective supervision.

Core Values	Respect, diversity, support, directed feedback, formative, summative, collaboration, courageous conversations.
Mission	Supervisors build teacher capacity.
Vision	All teachers value supervision.
Goals	Improvement of teaching and learning for teachers and students.
Key Strategies	Walk-throughs, clinical supervision, coaching, mentoring, dialogues, meaningful and directed feedback.
Key Indicators	Professional learning communities (PLCs).

Figure 1.3.   Examples of Key Performance Indicators for Supervision

Involving all teachers in the informational, formational, and transformational process of supervision should lead teachers to value supervision. Supervision provides collaboration (mentoring, clinical supervision, coaching, walk-throughs, directed and meaningful feedback) for all teachers. It allows teachers to talk to another adult about hopes, dreams, problems, and other concerns.

Teaching can be a lonely experience. Active collaborative supervision can reduce frustration within the profession. There are a great number of teachers who leave the profession in the first few years because of a lack of mentoring and support. Effective supervision can help to build confidence for a teacher experimenting with and learning new pedagogy. It can assist and support teachers as they grow in the art and craft of teaching.

Although many teachers and school leaders value supervision, there are others who do not. Various issues may arise that prohibit or impair the development of a supervision program. Some of these issues follow:

- What if the supervisor does not value the importance of supervision? If supervision is not important to the school leader, there is very little chance of supervision having an effect on teacher growth and increased student learning.
- What if the supervisor does not have the knowledge, skills, and disposition to be an effective supervisor? This raises the issue of quality professional learning for school leaders. Leaders and teachers must be appropriately schooled in what is effective supervision. There must be a common vocabulary.
- What if teachers see no value in supervision and they resist it? Some teachers will contend that supervision has made no difference in their teaching in the past, so why should they consider it now? How does a supervisor respond to this concern?
- How does supervision become meaningful and effective? What elements are necessary?
- How does a supervisor know the difference between supervision and evaluation and how does that supervisor instruct teachers about this difference?

A careful study of what constitutes effective teacher learning and growth will help to clarify these issues. The first part of the *Professional Learning and Growth Model* is a *supervision program* in which supervisors develop a professional relationship with teachers to support them in the work of teaching and learning. A relationship is formed by frequent visits to classrooms and conversations pertaining to what was observed. Part of this ongoing process involves a continual appraisal of teachers about their teaching competence and experiences.

Effective teachers are empowered to continue their own growth. New teachers and ineffective teachers are often offered many opportunities through such supervisory techniques as clinical supervision, walk-throughs, coaching, and mentoring to show growth. Although supervision is a continual process, generally evaluation is a summative process. It should be conducted according to state law and district policies governing teacher performance appraisal. Therefore, the second part of the Professional Learning and Growth Model includes the evaluation process.

DEFINING EVALUATION

Supervision is about supervisors helping teachers build their teaching skills and addressing the need for ongoing improvement, and evaluation is a related function that addresses decisions about performance. The supervisor builds a relationship with the teacher by frequent observations of and conversations with the teacher. Examples of teacher lesson plans and student work provide the data on the quality of teaching and learning in a teacher's classroom. The evaluator makes decisions about the quality of the performance and provides a rating in the process.

This stage in the Professional Learning and Growth Model emerges when supervisors make judgments on the quality of teaching based on what they have seen and heard in classrooms. Most states require by statute that teacher performance be evaluated and rated in public school districts. Therefore, this transition from supervisor to *evaluator* takes place as school leaders conduct comprehensive evaluations of teachers.

The evaluations can be formative or summative. *Formative evaluations* are ongoing discussions between the evaluator and the teacher for the purpose of professional learning. The evaluator gives the teacher directed and meaningful feedback on what was done well and what needs to be improved. *Summative evaluations* are discussions between the evaluator and teacher to provide a performance rating for purposes of continued employment, remediation, or dismissal.

School districts, superintendents, principals, and teachers must grapple with the purposes of evaluation. Some educators will say the purpose of evaluation is to ensure teacher quality. Based on established standards of effective teaching created by the district or state, evaluation is a measurement of how a teacher performs according to those expectations.

For teachers who meet these standards, their job may be secure. Teachers who do not meet these standards often are offered targeted assistance that includes strategies to meet the defined teaching standards. If these teachers are able to make changes in areas of weakness and show improvement, then their jobs may continue. For those teachers who do not meet the expectations, they may be terminated. There are myriads of factors that govern continued contractual employment, remediation, or dismissal depending on state laws, board policies, union contracts, and district evaluation procedures.

There are educators who believe that the purpose of evaluation is to encourage professional learning. Evaluators need to help teachers identify their strengths and weaknesses. These professional conversations empower teachers to grow so that student achievement increases. However, evaluation should do both. Evaluation must ensure quality teaching through performance review as well as continued professional learning and growth opportunities.

In a report titled *The Widget Effect* by Weisberg et al. (2009), problems with evaluation systems were researched. The report found that evaluations were often too infrequent. Conducted once a year or once every couple of years, the evaluations did not give meaningful feedback to teachers. Many veteran teachers were not evaluated for years. Evaluators lost out in the opportunity to help these teachers grow.

Many times, the evaluations were unfocused. Student learning was not addressed. Instead, evaluators used checklists focusing on classroom environment instead of instruction. Other times, the evaluations did not adequately distinguish between teacher ratings. There was a pass-or-fail judgment with most teachers being rated as pass. And yet, student academic scores were not rising. This provided a disconnect between teaching, learning, and student performance.

Another problem identified was that the experiences in this process were not helpful to teachers. Teachers were not given direct or meaningful feedback. As a result, they saw no value in the experience. Many teachers were compliant with the law and did the annual ritual with no signs of improvement.

Sometimes, evaluation was not a good experience for the teachers. They feared the experience and became defensive. Much of this was due to evaluators not building a trusting relationship with teachers. This fear and defensiveness were also attributed to ineffective evaluation procedures or teachers themselves who do not see the value in ongoing professional learning.

As a result of these shortcomings in the traditional evaluation systems and the impetus of the U.S. Department of Education competition called *Race to the Top*, states have made changes to their evaluation systems. Examples include the *Performance Evaluation Reform Act* (PERA, 2010) in Illinois, the *Ohio Teacher Evaluation System* (OTES, 2014), and the *Oregon Matrix* (2014).

Evaluations in most of these states have four components. Standards of professional practice present a vision of effective teaching. Performance levels of teachers are differentiated into four categories. Evaluations of teachers are determined by multiple measures such as evidence of professional practice, professional responsibilities, and student learning and growth. Frequent evaluations are accompanied by professional learning activities.

Another effort to address the problem of teacher evaluations is the growing idea that evidence of a teacher's contributions to student learning should be a major component of teacher evaluation systems. *Value-added models* (VAMs) suggest that student achievement gain should be linked to a specific teacher. The student gain is supposed to be reflective of a teacher's effectiveness. Most research has concluded that value-added models should not be the primary measure of evaluating teachers.

A further approach to teacher evaluation has been the growth of standards-based evaluation processes. A clear example of this type of approach is the *Interstate Teacher Assessment and Support Consortium* (InTASC) standards (see appendix A). More about this process and these standards can be found in chapter 2.

The *New Teacher Project* (2010) presented six design standards that need to be part of meaningful and effective evaluations. All teachers should be evaluated yearly. There should be clear and rigorous expectations of teaching that lead to increased student learning. Multiple measures of performance must be considered. Evaluations should use four or five ratings to accommodate differentiation in teachers. Frequent observations by evaluators should lead to constructive feedback to teachers. Evaluations must matter as key factors in retaining or dismissing teachers.

School district evaluation processes must create key goals for effective evaluation. The number one goal must focus on evaluations that lead to improved student learning. The second goal requires a definition of effective teaching. The definition must clearly explain what teachers need to know and be able to do in working with students. The third goal must be the establishment of continual professional learning for all teachers throughout their careers.

School districts must establish clear purposes for evaluation to become meaningful. The process must identify ways to strengthen the knowledge, skills, dispositions, and practices of teachers so that student performance increases. The processes must support professional learning activities and plans. For school evaluators, there are several guiding principles to understand the full effect of teacher evaluation.

1. Know what your state requires for evaluations. This means attending professional development sessions that lead to certification or endorsements in that state in order to evaluate. Usually state laws

explain procedures and specific dates in determining when teachers need to be evaluated.

2. Know your district's policies and procedures for teacher evaluation. This means knowing what models of teacher evaluation are being followed and how to implement them.
3. Provide teachers with what they need to know about the evaluation system's core content (standards of excellence and levels of performance) and how it will be implemented (the specifics of dates, meeting times, people involved, and required documentation).
4. Build relationships with teachers through relevant supervision activities that include frequent observations and meaningful conversations with them about their lesson plans and student work. Build trust. Once this happens, teachers may become more open to directed and meaningful feedback.

Figure 1.4 provides examples of these key performance indicators for an evaluation program. A deeper examination of teacher evaluation is found in chapter 6.

Core Values	Honesty, courageous conversations, collaboration, professional growth, the good of children.
Mission	Formative and summative evaluations ensure quality professional learning and growth development activities.
Vision	All formative and summative evaluations will lead to increased quality assurance and professional development in all teachers.
Goals	Teachers will use evaluation as a tool to deepen areas of strength and to work on areas in need of improvement.
Key Strategies	Frequent formative feedback and conversations between supervisors and teachers.
Key Indicators	Increased student achievement and effective teachers.

Figure 1.4.   Examples of Key Performance Indicators for Evaluation

In the Professional Learning and Growth Model, the first two elements are supervision and evaluation. Supervision is the development of a relationship in which the supervisor and teacher work together to build increased teaching and learning experiences for the teacher and even more so for the students. A supervisor will visit, encourage, support, and challenge teachers to grow so that they will be successful with students. All of these activities provide a supervisor with an ongoing picture of where the teacher is at in terms of professional competence.

This leads to the second part of the Professional Learning and Growth Model in which the supervisor must make a judgment about the teacher.

A formative judgment is done through directed and meaningful feedback, and encourages the teacher to seek further growth through professional learning. A summative judgment ensures accountability and says this teacher is either competent, in need of remediation, or must be dismissed. Figure 1.5 shows the differences between supervision and evaluation and how they work together to ensure effective teaching.

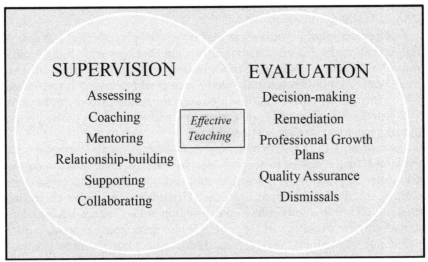

Figure 1.5.   The Elements of Supervision and Evaluation for Effective Teaching

DEFINING PROFESSIONAL LEARNING

Once a supervisor has spent time in teacher capacity building and providing teachers with meaningful formative and summative evaluations, the next task is to work with the teachers to help them maximize their strengths and address their areas in need of improvement. This leads to the formation of an action plan in which the teacher focuses on areas of continued growth. Most teachers are familiar with the term *professional development,* and they know that their school or district will provide time throughout the year in which they are to learn. Teachers have had their share of good and poor quality professional development activities.

Professional development includes all those learning experiences at the end of the day, the meetings after an early dismissal, a before-school meeting with a late start schedule, the all-day workshops, or the regularly scheduled professional learning community meetings during the day and faculty meetings. Every teacher can relate to these experiences.

Through the efforts of the *Learning Forward* organization, a shift has occurred in professional development. The redefined focus is on *professional learning.* Although teachers may need those professional development days or events focused on specific skills, there is more to consider about continued learning and growth.

Professional learning is not just a one-day event but is a process of continually learning. Teachers need to think about lifelong learning and how it affects their practice and day-to-day student learning. Every day, teachers can improve their practice, which will have a long-term effect as student learning increases.

Another national organization that promotes professional learning is the *Association for Supervision and Curriculum Development* (ASCD). ASCD publishes practical books for school leaders and teachers. In addition to these books, a monthly journal, titled *Educational Leadership,* is published, which focuses on current issues in education. ASCD also offers regional and yearly conferences to enrich educators and assist them in their ongoing professional learning and growth.

Croft et al. (2010) researched *job-embedded professional development* and explained that it refers to teacher learning that is grounded in day-to-day teaching practices. It is learning that is designed to enhance teachers' content-specific instructional practices. The intent is to improve student learning. Job-embedded professional development is classroom based, integrated into the workday, and shared. It is also an ongoing process, inquiry based, and aligned with state standards and school improvement goals.

Formats for job-embedded learning can include action research, case discussions, coaching, critical friend groups, and data teams. Job-embedded learning can also encompass examining student work, lesson studies, mentoring, portfolios, study groups, and implementing individual professional growth plans.

Professional development can include a variety of activities. It is a broad, encompassing term. There are *in-service activities* of one- or two-day workshops in which teachers are trained by content experts on some topic that must be implemented by all teachers throughout the district. This may include activities such as technology; special education initiatives such as *response to intervention* (RtI); the common core standards; or some other state, federal, or district mandates.

Professional development may focus on developing the expertise of teachers in problem-solving and action research. Teachers work collegially throughout the school year to research, address, and create solutions to issues unique to their school. *Renewal activities* are ongoing personal growth opportunities in which teachers engage to reflect, renew, and reinvent their teaching practices and styles.

There is a need for each of these activities at particular times and for varied purposes. There is also a need for supervisors to encourage teachers to go beyond what was called professional development to what is now redefined as professional learning. Instead of professional development being conducted by the district or school for teachers, it now becomes an individual responsibility for a teacher to take ownership for professional learning.

The supervisor guides teachers by providing opportunities to develop within a teacher learning and growth model. The model includes a relevant supervision and evaluation plan that is facilitated by an individual, a school, and a district professional development plan. The goal is to improve teaching and learning. The outcome should be improved student performance.

Professional learning needs to be evaluated to ensure its effectiveness. Kirkpatrick and Kirkpatrick (2007) suggest that there are four levels of evaluation of professional development: *reaction, learning, transfer,* and *results*. *Reaction* concerns whether participants are satisfied with what they experienced. *Learning* centers on determining whether participants used their learning in their classroom experiences. The *results* focus on how this learning and *transfer* have an effect on student learning.

Various issues arise in teacher professional learning. Can a school district afford professional learning? What criteria determine the creation, implementation, and evaluation of professional learning? Who determines the when and where of professional learning? How do school leaders deal with a teacher who resists participation in professional learning? Figure 1.6 provides examples of these key performance indicators for a professional learning program. A more detailed account of professional learning can be found in chapter 4.

Core Values	Continuous improvement, collaboration, lifelong learning.
Mission	Professional learning and growth as an ongoing process for teachers.
Vision	All teachers will participate in ongoing learning and growth opportunities.
Goals	Sustained and ongoing teacher growth.
Key Strategies	Development of individual teacher learning and growth plans.
Key Indicators	Active involvement of teachers in their individual learning and growth plans.

Figure 1.6.   Examples of Key Performance Indicators for Professional Learning

SUMMARY

A history of supervision, evaluation, and professional learning shows us that there have been varied approaches to effective teaching and learning. We stand on the shoulders of such giants as Mann, Dewey, Hunter,

Danielson, Marzano, and Marshall as we move forward to improve teaching and learning for the teacher and even more so for our students.

Supervision, evaluation, and professional learning are key elements of a Professional Learning and Growth Model. Supervision involves the supervisor building ongoing relationships with all teachers to encourage, support, direct, challenge, and oversee the process of teaching and learning in the school. Supervisors have the task of using the best form of supervision to meet the needs of the teacher so there is growth.

Evaluation is the process of supervisors making judgments about the quality of teaching, which leads to professional learning. Formative evaluations help teachers identify strengths and areas in need of improvement. Summative evaluations provide evidence of whether a teacher should continue teaching or move on to another job.

Professional learning is the process of lifelong learning for teachers. It can be a one-day in-service, a series of professional development opportunities, or an ongoing series of experiences for teacher renewal and growth.

CASE STUDY

You have accepted the appointment as the new principal of Smithville Middle School. At a meeting with the entire faculty, you must provide an overview of the new supervision, evaluation, and professional learning program that will be implemented in the current year. Create a PowerPoint presentation for these teachers with highlights of the new program. How will you invite the teachers to discuss the implementation of this program and begin the conversation about effective teaching?

EXERCISES AND DISCUSSION QUESTIONS

1. Share your experiences of supervision, evaluation, and professional learning. What were the positive and negative aspects of each?
2. Interview a school leader about his or her experiences in supervision, evaluation, and professional learning.
3. How do we help teachers understand the difference between formative and summative evaluation?
4. What makes a professional learning experience valuable? When is it not valuable?
5. Reflect on and explain how your district has or has not integrated a Professional Learning and Growth Model in supervision and evaluation.

6. In reading and reflecting on the history of supervision, evaluation, and professional learning, what can we learn from these experiences?

REFERENCES

Council of Chief State Officers. (2013). *Model core teaching standards and learning progressions for teachers 1.0: A resource for ongoing teacher development*. Washington, DC: Interstate Teacher Assessment and Support Consortium (InTASC).

Croft, A., Coggshall, J., Dolan, M., Powers, E., & Killion, J. (2010). *Job embedded professional development: What it is, who is responsible, and how to get it done well*. Washington, DC: National Comprehensive Center for Teacher Quality.

Danielson, C. (2007). *Enhancing professional practice: A framework for teaching*. (2nd ed.). Alexandria, VA: Association for Supervision and Curriculum Development.

Danielson, C., & McGreal, T. (2000). *Teacher evaluation to enhance professional practice*. Alexandria, VA: Association for Supervision and Curriculum Development.

Educational Leadership Consortium Council. (2011). *ELCC Standards*. Washington, DC: National Policy Board for Educational Administration (NPBEA).

Hunter, M. (1980). Six types of supervisory conferences. *Educational Leadership, 37*(5), 408–412.

Interstate School Leaders Licensure Consortium. (2011). *ISLLC Standards*. Washington, DC: Interstate School Leaders Licensure Consortium of Chief State School Officers.

Kirkpatrick, D., & Kirkpatrick, J. (2007). *Implementing the four levels*. San Francisco, CA: Berrett-Koehler Publishers.

Marzano, R. (2012). The two purposes of teacher evaluation. *Educational Leadership, 70*(3), 14–19.

Marzano, R., Waters, R., & McNulty, B. (2005). *School leadership that works: From research to results*. Alexandria, VA: Association for Supervision and Curriculum Development and Mid-Continental Research for Education and Learning.

The New Teacher Project. (2010). *Teacher evaluation 2.0*. Brooklyn, NY: The New Teacher Project.

No Child Left Behind (NCLB) Act of 2001, Pub. L. No. 107-110, § 115, Stat. 1425 (2002).

Ohio Teacher Evaluation System. (2014). http://www.education.ohio.gov

Oregon Department of Education. (2014). http://www.ode.state.or.ush

Performance Evaluation Reform Act (PERA). (2010). Education Reform in Illinois. State of Illinois.

Race to the Top (RTTT) Act of 2011. (2011). https://www.govtrack.us/congress/bills/112/hr1532

Taylor, F. (1911). *The principles of scientific management*. New York, NY: Harper and Brothers.

Weisberg, D., Sexton, S., Mulhern, J., Keeling, D., Schunk, J., Palcisco, A., & Morgan, K. (2009). *The widget effect: Our national failure to acknowledge and act on differences in teacher effectiveness* (2nd ed.). The New Teacher Project.

Whitehead, M. (1952). Teachers look at supervision. *Educational Leadership,10*(2), 1011–1106.

Wise, A., Darling-Hammond, L., McLaughlin, M., & Bernstein, H. (1984). *Teacher evaluation: A study of effective evaluation practices.* Santa Monica, CA: RAND Corporation.

2

✛

Standards and Models for Teacher Evaluation

OBJECTIVES

At the conclusion of this chapter you will be able to:

1. Learn the importance of and reasons for national, state, and professional teaching standards (ELCC 1, 2, 4, 5, 6; ISLLC 1, 2, 3, 4, 5, 6; TLEC 1, 2, 3, 4, 5; InTASC 1, 2, 3, 4, 5, 6, 7, 8, 9, 10; Learning Forward Standards).
2. Compare several frameworks of supervision and evaluation (ELCC 1, 2, 3, 4, 5, 6; ISLLC 1, 2, 3, 4, 5, 6; TLEC 1, 2, 3, 4, 5; InTASC 1, 2, 3, 4, 5, 6, 7, 8, 9, 10; Learning Forward Standards).
3. Understand and use a professional learning and growth model for performance evaluations (ELCC 1, 2, 3, 4, 5, 6; ISLLC 1, 2, 3, 4, 5, 6; TLEC 1, 2, 3, 4, 5; InTASC 1, 2, 3, 4, 5, 6, 7, 8, 9, 10; Learning Forward Standards).

FEDERAL, STATE, AND PROFESSIONAL TEACHING STANDARDS

Even though states have the responsibility to oversee education, the federal government has affected education through various acts of legislation and programs. Three initiatives have encouraged educators to redefine quality teaching, which have led to the development of national standards. These federal initiatives are the *Elementary and Secondary Education Act*, *No Child Left Behind* (2001), and *Race to the Top* (2011). Each initiative has had a significant effect on educational policy and funding since its enactment into federal law.

Federal Initiatives

Elementary and Secondary Act

The Elementary and Secondary Education Act (ESEA) was signed into law on April 11, 1965. This act was part of President Johnson's *War on Poverty* legislation. Reauthorized every five years, the goals are to ensure equal access to education for all students, set high standards for academic importance, and demand a rigorous level of accountability from schools and districts.

Federal money is given to states for programs for struggling learners, migrant students, rural educational initiatives, Advanced Placement (AP), Limited English Proficiency (LEP) students, 21st Century Learning, protection of homeless students, career and technical education, school safety, protection against discrimination, and private schools. The federal government checks compliance in these programs by yearly monitoring.

Title II, Part A focuses on increasing academic achievement of all students by helping schools and districts improve teacher and principal quality. It also requires state agencies to document all teachers as highly qualified. Federal monies can be used for teacher preparation and the qualification of new teachers, recruitment and hiring, induction programs, professional development, and retention. Funds also can be used to improve the skills and knowledge of principals for effective school leadership.

These federal monies helped school districts to concentrate on teacher growth through professional learning opportunities. In addition to this, federal monies have also been used to increase the skills and competencies of school leaders. Standards began to emerge at both the national and state levels to give voice to what students should know and be able to demonstrate. In most states, curriculum has been articulated and aligned with these standards.

No Child Left Behind

The No Child Left Behind (NCLB) legislation signed into law by President George H. W. Bush on January 8, 2002, was a reauthorization of the ESEA. The Act was intended to close the achievement gap with accountability and flexibility of school choice. It set high standards and established measurable goals that could improve student learning. Each state was asked to design assessments in basic skills that would be administered annually to show academic progress with school report cards. The intent was to improve the quality of each school and to help students learn and perform at higher levels.

For students to meet this academic progress, it was imperative that teachers and school leaders increase their skills. National standards for teacher and school leaders began to emerge. The Interstate Teacher Assessment and Support Consortium (InTASC) Model Core Teaching Standards and the Interstate School Leaders Licensure Consortium (ISLLC; 2011) leadership standards are examples of these national standards and will be discussed later in this chapter.

Race to the Top

Race to the Top (RTTT) was a four-billion-dollar grant offered by the U.S. Department of Education to spur innovation and reform at the state and local levels. This grant was funded by the *American Recovery and Reinvestment Act of 2009*. This initiative was established by the Obama administration on July 24, 2009. RTTT was meant to further advance the original goals of the NCLB and to encourage states to increase accountability and student performance levels.

To qualify for the monies available, states needed to demonstrate that they had developed performance-based standards. States had to be in compliance with the *Common Core Standards*. These states also had to be willing to turn around the lowest performing schools. Further, qualifying states had to create data systems. Additionally, these states had to provide evidence of creating high-quality teacher and school leader programs. Finally, these states had to establish benchmark state success factors.

The requirements of the RTTT program resulted in many states revising their teacher and principal evaluation processes. In an effort to ensure excellent teachers and principals, these new programs were more demanding and comprehensive than previous evaluation programs. One of the greatest shifts has been the use of student learning gains as part of a teacher's yearly evaluation.

Besides the federal laws affecting education, there have been standards-based initiatives that have also contributed to the improvement of the quality of teaching. One is InTASC, and the other is the *National Board for Professional Teaching Standards* (1989). Each of these organizations is concerned about teacher quality, effective supervision, evaluation, and coming to a shared knowledge and common language of what constitutes effective teaching.

Interstate Teacher Assessment and Support Consortium

In 1987, the Council of Chief State School Officers (CCSSO; 2013) created the Interstate Teacher Assessment and Support Consortium (InTASC). The council comprised state education agencies and national educational organizations. It had a dual purpose: (1) reform the preparation, licensing, and ongoing professional development of teachers and (2) ensure quality teaching to increase student learning and performance. Originally designed to model core teaching standards for new teachers, the InTASC standards have been revised to include opportunities for veteran teachers to improve as well. The standards outline the knowledge, dispositions, and performances that effective teachers should know and be able to demonstrate. What makes InTASC so significant is that many state models of effective teaching are based on these standards. As such, these standards are a foundational work. The InTASC standards can be found in appendix A of this book.

There are three stated purposes for the InTASC standards. First, the standards create a larger context for the vision of what effective teaching should become in schools and classrooms. Second, the standards define a specific level of performance that must be met. Third, the standards articulate the opportunities necessary for a teacher to meet these standards.

The InTASC standards are organized into four general categories, which lay a foundation for a vision of quality teaching. The first category is about the *learner and learning*. The three standards under this category are *learner development, learning differences,* and *learning environments*. What makes this category significant is that it starts with the needs of the learner and recognizes that teachers need to take into account learner differences and the effect the environment can have on learning.

The second category is *content*. The two standards under this are content knowledge and application. In this category, the content of curriculum is highlighted. Teachers not only need to be aware of what they need to teach but also how this content can be applied. Curriculum is not only content. It is also about using information to solve problems students encounter.

The third category is *instructional practices*. This category includes assessment of learning, planning for instruction, and instructional strategies. Teachers need to administer or develop assessments so they know that the students have learned. Good planning increases the quality of teaching. A variety of instructional strategies also adds to the quality of the lesson.

The fourth category is *professional responsibility*. The two standards under this category are professional learning and ethical practice, leadership, and collaboration. The first emphasizes the importance of *ongoing learning* for quality teaching and learning. Ethical practice, the second, underscores the necessity of teachers doing the right things for students.

In the tenth standard under this category, teachers are encouraged to become *teacher leaders* in the school. The concept of teacher leaders is a growing movement in schools today because these teachers lead growth in content areas and within grade levels. Teacher leaders are active members of the leadership team, and they are often involved in the coaching and mentoring of their colleagues.

What makes the InTASC standards so unique is that they now include learning progressions for teachers. The learning progressions are used as support tools for teacher development. Although evaluation systems identify areas in need of improvement, they do not include helpful support tools. These learning progressions articulate a continuum of growth and, thus, give teachers the experience of seeing what effective practice looks like. The standards include suggested professional learning activities.

National Board for Professional Teaching Standards

In 1987, based on a document titled "What Teachers Should Know and Be Able to Do," the National Board for Professional Teaching Standards (NBPTS) articulated the *Five Propositions of Accomplished Teaching and Their Indicators*. This document provides a vision of accomplished teaching that includes knowledge, skills, and dispositions that characterize *national board certified teachers*. The Five Propositions of Accomplished Teaching are outlined in figure 2.1.

1. Accomplished teachers are committed to students and their learning.
2. Accomplished teachers know the subjects they teach and how to teach these subjects to students.
3. Accomplished teachers are responsible for managing and monitoring student learning.
4. Accomplished teachers think systematically about their practice and learn from experiences.
5. Accomplished teachers are members of learning communities.

Figure 2.1. The Five Propositions of Accomplished Teaching (NBPTS, 2014)

The NBPTS suggest a process of growth and assessment for teachers. Teachers submit a portfolio of their work that includes lesson plans, samples of student work, and videos of classroom teaching. A lengthy reflection paper on the process of teaching and learning that shows evidence of student learning is also required. At the conclusion of the process, teachers take a written assessment. Teachers who pass this strenuous process become board certified and are considered among the best teachers in the country. Some districts offer pay incentives for teachers who undergo this process.

The InTASC standards and the NBPTS suggest visions of excellent teaching that lead to increased student achievement. Around the same time these standards were offered, two other sets of standards were developed to define the qualities of effective leaders. Developed in the 1990s, the Interstate School Leaders Licensure Consortium (ISLLC) and the Educational Leadership Constituent Council (ELCC; 2011) standards complement the effective teaching standards by defining the qualities, skills, and dispositions of effective leadership.

Supporting the ELCC and ISLLC standards is a strong research base in leadership factors and traits. Strong, effective, school leadership has proven to have a significant effect on student learning and performance. Leaders influence student learning by improving the quality of each teacher through the supervision and evaluation processes. Leaders are second only to teachers in having an effect on student learning.

Interstate School Leaders Licensure Consortium

The Interstate School Leaders Licensure Consortium (ISLLC) standards are another initiative of the Council of Chief School Officers (CCSSO), a national organization of public school officials from all fifty states. They developed a set of common standards that provide a vision of what school leadership should be for practicing school leaders.

Each of the six standards has knowledge, performance, and disposition indicators that attest to effective leadership to promote the success of all students. University leadership programs and many state departments of education have adopted these standards as guiding principles for accreditation of training programs.

A *vision of learning* is the first standard. Effective leaders must work with teachers and community stakeholders to develop a clear understanding about what the core values and purposes of the school are. It takes time to create, write, implement, and evaluate this vision. But once the vision is established and there is shared ownership, it brings everyone together to achieve a common goal for learning.

Closely associated with vision is the second standard of promoting a positive *school culture.* Culture provides the values or important building blocks for teachers to thrive and students to achieve. It involves developing an effective instructional program, applying best practices, and designing relevant and ongoing professional learning activities for all teachers. Related to this is the *climate* of the school. Climate is often used interchangeably with culture. However, climate is more about creating a warm, welcoming environment that can lead to teacher and student success.

Management of the organization, including operations and resources, is the third standard. An effective leader has to be attuned to these business aspects of the school. This area of leadership keeps all systems of the school functioning smoothly. To ignore these areas is to jeopardize the teaching and learning programs.

Collaboration with families and the local community is the fourth standard. Effective leaders must communicate with parents and other members of the local community. The leader helps to ensure a good learning environment for teachers and students by developing positive relationships with all stakeholders.

Trust and respect is the fifth standard. Effective leaders must be ethical, fair, and honest. All people must be respected. Some schools develop a code of ethics for teachers. Appropriate behavior must be demanded of all adults and students. Many schools develop a discipline program for students such as the *Positive Behavior Intervention System* (PBIS) or a positive attitude program such as *Character Counts.* Bullying, a huge issue in schools today, cannot be tolerated. So programs to help prevent such behaviors are developed. This standard directly affects standard two regarding culture.

The sixth standard focuses on the *larger political, social, legal, religious, and economic context* of the school and the world. Schools are part of a larger world. Effective leaders must understand the school role in the larger context and be able to respond accordingly. A real danger for school leaders is losing sight of the larger context and becoming isolated.

The ISLLC standards were revised in 2008. The new version gives a vision of what school leaders should know and be able to do in effective school leadership practices. Some school districts use these standards as the criteria for performance evaluation for school leaders such as principals, assistant principals, deans, superintendents, and central office personnel.

Educational Leadership Constituent Council Standards

In 2002, the Educational Leadership Constituent Council (ELCC) on behalf of the National Council for Accreditation of Teacher Education (NCATE) and the National Policy Board for Educational Administration

(NPBEA) developed a set of standards to review and provide criteria for the accreditation of university school administration preparation programs. The ELCC aligned its standards to match the ISLLC standards. The standards are similar in content. Both sets of standards are meant for aspiring and practicing school leaders.

The ELCC standards are different from the ISLLC standards in that they are performance-based expectations for school leaders in training whereas the ISLLC standards are performance-based expectations for practicing school leaders. Students in graduate leadership programs at universities must show evidence of competent performances of these standards. In a yearlong internship program of leadership, graduate students must log hours of experiences in these standards within classroom and school building settings. The ISLLC standards are in appendix B of this book. The ELLC Standards are in appendix C of this book.

State Professional Teaching Standards

Additional initiatives that have had a significant effect on teacher performance standards are those at the state level. Figure 2.2 provides a partial example of the State of Illinois State Professional Teaching Standards (2013). Standards such as these also help to define and categorize performance expectations.

Standard 1 - Teaching Diverse Students–*The competent teacher understands the diverse characteristics and abilities of each student and how individuals develop and learn within the context of their social, economic, cultural, linguistic, and academic experiences. The teacher uses these experiences to create instructional opportunities that maximize student learning.*

Knowledge Indicators–The competent teacher:
1A) understands the spectrum of student diversity (e.g., race and ethnicity, socioeconomic status, special education, gifted, English language learners (ELL), sexual orientation, gender, gender identity) and the assets that each student brings to learning across the curriculum.

Performance Indicators–The competent teacher:
1H) analyzes and uses student information to design instruction that meets the diverse needs of students and leads to ongoing growth and achievement.

Figure 2.2.   Partial Example of Illinois Professional Teacher Standards (2013)

State standards address the importance of quality classroom teaching. Such teaching is critical to producing high levels of student learning and performance. The standards provide a guide for teachers at all stages of their careers to reflect on their teaching and to seek ways to improve that teaching. In each of the standards, there are many elements and further explanations of what teachers should know, think, and do to be effective teachers.

In Table 2.1, note the similarities and differences in the professional state standards for the teaching profession in New York, Ohio, and California. Each state stresses the importance of understanding students and knowing the diversity within the classrooms. Knowledge of course content is required in each state. Assessment is also a high priority. Knowing good instructional strategies is also important. The learning environment is highlighted. Professional growth and collaboration are also a part of quality teaching.

These sample state professional teaching standards provide teachers with a road map of what knowledge and skills are evidence of effective teaching. In addition to this, the standards can provide areas of growth to develop in a professional learning plan for individual teachers, for all the teachers of the school, or all the teachers of the district.

Table 2.1.   Comparison of Professional Teaching Standards

State Standards	New York	Ohio	California
1	Knowledge of students and learning	Students	Engaging and supporting all students in learning
2	Knowledge of content and instructional planning	Content	Creating and maintaining effective environments for student learning
3	Instructional practice	Assessment	Understanding and organizing subject matter for learning
4	Learning environment	Instruction	Planning and designing instruction learning experiences for students
5	Assessment for student learning	Learning environment	Assessing student learning
6	Professional responsibilities and collaboration	Collaboration and communication	Developing a professional educator
7	Professional growth	Professional responsibilities and growth	N/A

Source: Based on an interpretation of the New York, Ohio, and California Professional Teaching Standards.

As states have developed professional teaching standards to describe quality teaching, some states have mandated local school districts to select teacher evaluation systems that will meet their local needs. Models are a central part of the new teacher evaluation laws that require districts to use an evaluation system that will accurately measure teacher performance.

In Illinois, the new law is called the *Performance Evaluation Reform Act* (PERA) based on Senate Bill 315, Public Act 96-0861. PERA was passed by the Illinois General Assembly and signed by the governor in January 2010. Implementation of the law was done over a three-year period. Many other states have also passed similar laws that provide evidence to the U.S. Department of Education that they can compete for *Race to the Top* federal monies to improve education in their states.

Evaluation

MODELS OF PROFESSIONAL TEACHER EVALUATION
influence state systems

Three common models of teacher evaluation go by the last names of their developers. The three models are those created by Charlotte Danielson, Robert Marzano, and Kim Marshall. Their models were created to respond to concerns with traditional evaluation systems.

Danielson (2007) believed that many of the traditional systems were inconsistent. Evaluation systems did not differentiate between novice teachers and more experienced teachers. A lack of precision in the system rendered most teachers as excellent. Very few teachers received a poor evaluation. If they did, they were moved from school to school instead of receiving mentoring and coaching that would help them to become more effective teachers.

Evaluations were also a monologue in which the evaluator did all the work and no feedback was solicited from the teacher. In addition to this, there were no shared ideas of good teaching or a common language to direct conversations to professional learning. As a result, many teachers were passive and not lifelong learners pursuing continual improvement.

Marshall (2013) also claimed that traditional systems of evaluation did not significantly improve teaching and student learning. Principals spent very little time evaluating teachers. The evaluation consisted of a biannual forty-five-minute observation with a running narrative of what was observed. Little to no constructive feedback was given to teachers. So, how could this be an accurate evaluation?

When principals did come to evaluate, the teacher was notified ahead of time. Many teachers put on a *dog-and-pony show*. That is, they presented their best lessons. This, however, was not typical of their daily teaching experience. After the once-a-year visit, the teacher went back to normal routines, and the principal put the evaluation report into the teacher's file.

No difference in teaching and learning happened. It was merely a procedural event that had to be done to satisfy state and local district mandates.

The once-a-year visit by the principal did change the classroom dynamics, however. Students often behaved better because of the presence of the principal. This is why frequent visits by the principal, such as walkthroughs, would give the principal a more accurate picture of the typical day in the classroom.

The presence of the principal would be typical in the everyday events of the classroom, and the principal could observe more typical student behavior rather than behavior that would occur if the principal were present only once or twice a year.

Another inconsistency in traditional systems of evaluation was the fact that principals were required to complete detailed write-ups. Very often, principals were so busy writing what they saw and heard that they missed the whole picture of teaching and learning. They would get focused on a few things rather than on the whole process. Sometimes the evaluation forms were so legalistic and cumbersome that the evaluators would get lost in the checklists and the jargon.

Often principals were in such a hurry to get the evaluations done that they did not put in more effort to make the evaluations meaningful. These principals had too many other things to do that seemed more important. At other times, the principal did not want to take the time to confront less-than-adequate teaching. These principals wanted to keep the peace and avoid the long battles of remediation and dealing with the union or district lawyer.

All of these reasons suggest why a new type of teacher evaluation system was needed. In addition to this, the key point was that teachers were not growing. These evaluations did not make a difference in their teaching and learning. Even more so, mediocre or bad teachers were allowed to stay, which negatively affected students.

Students have to be the central focus of teaching and learning. New systems of teacher evaluations need to invite teachers to grow so that student learning increases. There is a direct correlation between effective teaching and student achievement. It is an issue of equity.

Charlotte Danielson (2007) developed her *Framework for Teaching* to address the importance of professional learning and accurate documentation of teacher performance. She stated that evaluation should be linked to the mission of the school district. Further, the continual process of evaluation should be linked to professional learning and supervision. Danielson maintains that evaluation also should include formative and summative evaluations that lead to professional conversations and coaching. Resources for the system to work properly need to be provided by schools and school districts.

The *Framework for Teaching* provides discussions about teaching between the evaluator and the teacher. Based on these discussions, the teacher needs to self-reflect by evaluating personal experiences and classroom methodology. Continual improvement of teaching becomes the norm. The framework is also aligned to InTASC; the National Council of Accreditation of Teacher Evaluation (NCATE), now renamed Council for the Accreditation of Educator Preparation (CAEP, 2012); and the National Board for Professional Teaching Standards (NBPTS) national standards.

The *Framework for Teaching* addresses the major themes of teaching. Divided into four domains, the framework has twenty-two components and seventy-six elements. The four domains are Planning and Preparation, Classroom Environment, Instruction, and Professional Responsibilities. The four domains show the alignment with the InTASC and several state professional standards for the teaching profession.

For the *Framework for Teaching* to have an effect, there needs to be attention to a clear definition of each of the domains, components, and elements. This means that teachers need to be given professional learning opportunities where they have time to learn the content of the framework and how it will be implemented in their districts.

In the *Framework for Teaching*, there is a four-level rating scale for teacher performance. Based on evidence of what is seen and heard in each of the four domains, teachers can be rated as *unsatisfactory, basic, proficient*, or *distinguished*. Teachers also need to have professional learning sessions where they come to understand the levels of performance and know what these levels look like in practice.

Evaluators also need professional learning opportunities where they learn the domains of the framework and the levels of performance and how to apply these in practice. The goal is to empower supervisors to make fair and consistent judgments based on evidence of what is seen and heard. In Illinois, in the *Growth Through Learning* and *Teachscape* online training programs, participants take five modules that prepare them to be approved to conduct evaluations of teachers. Evaluators must pass a test on domains two and three of the *Framework for Teaching*.

It is the responsibility of each state and school district to determine how it will apply a teaching framework to its particular circumstances. In Illinois, school districts are required to use a four-level scoring guide for teacher performance. For those districts that use the *Framework for Teaching*, the performance level rating words have been changed to *unsatisfactory, needs improvement, proficient*, and *excellent*. In the *Framework for Teaching*, the levels are described as *unsatisfactory, basic, proficient*, and *distinguished*.

Illinois is also one of the states that do not require the *Framework for Teaching* to be the sole model used. Other models of teacher evaluation may be chosen and even district developed to implement the teacher evaluation system. Some Illinois districts do not use the *Framework for Teaching*. For example, some districts use the Marzano *Causal Teacher Evaluation Model*.

The *Framework for Teaching* (Danielson & McGreal, 2000) also has three levels of evaluations that reflect the different stages of teacher growth. For the beginner teacher, track one includes induction, mentoring, and other supports to assist novice teachers as they learn to navigate all the dimensions of teaching as expressed in the four domains of the framework.

For experienced teachers, track two of evaluation centers on collaboration with other teachers, self-evaluation, and the development of a professional learning plan. Most teachers would be in this track. From this track, teacher leaders emerge as mentors, literary and math coaches, and grade-level team leaders.

Veteran teachers experiencing difficulties become part of track three and are given targeted assistance. A specific plan is developed for these teachers. They must provide evidence of improvement. If this fails, they may be asked to leave the profession.

A unique dimension to the Danielson framework is the offering of frameworks for special positions. Although the framework is designed for classroom teachers, Danielson also adjusted the framework for instructional specialists (coaches), library and media specialists, school nurses, school counselors, school psychologists, and therapeutic specialists.

The Marzano system of teacher evaluation is called the *Causal Teacher Evaluation Model*. The model identifies a direct cause-and-effect relationship between elements in the model and student learning. Teachers are given clear expectations and feedback that enables them to lead their own professional learning.

There are four domains. Domain one is classroom strategies and behaviors. Domain two is preparing and planning. Domain three is reflecting and teaching. Domain four is collegiality and professionalism. These domains are based in the national and state teacher professional standards. The domains also seem similar to those of the *Framework for Teaching*. But, there are key differences.

Domain one contains forty-one of the sixty elements included across the domains. It addresses what teachers do in the classroom. This domain is the most complex and has a direct causal link with student achievement. In domain one, there are nine design questions that are further organized into three major categories that reflect the complexity of teaching.

Domain two describes eight elements that center on planning and preparing for teaching. Domain three is focused on deliberate practice based on evaluations that leads to professional growth in areas in need of improvement. Teachers select an area to engage in in focused practice with feedback from self-reflection, peers, and supervisors. There are five elements addressed in this domain.

Domains one, two, and three contain fifty-four elements that specifically focus on increasing student achievement. In domain one, the focus is on classroom strategies and behaviors that lead to increased student achievement. To support that student achievement, there has to be good planning and preparation, which is described in domain two. Also, to support student achievement, there is a need for teachers to reflect on teaching that leads to self-improvement, which is the topic of domain three. These three domains are the direct causal chain that increases student achievement.

Domain four is not part of the causal chain. It invites teachers to consider the need for collegiality and professionalism. There are six elements addressed in this domain. Teachers are expected to participate in observing other teachers, collaborative lesson study sessions, teacher-led professional learning, and professional learning communities. All of this is for the purpose of student learning. Teachers should be able to see how specific teaching strategies affect student learning.

What makes the *Causal Teacher Evaluation Model* so unique is the emphasis on specific classroom strategies and behaviors that have a direct effect on student learning. This specificity leads to deliberate practice and the development of expertise. This differs from the *Framework for Teaching* model, which addresses more general areas.

The *Causal Teacher Evaluation Model* is based on the aggregation of research on elements that have been shown to correlate with student academic achievement and is based on thousands of studies over the past thirty-five years. Currently, there are many other studies being conducted by teachers in their classrooms on the effectiveness of specific strategies and student achievement.

Used by schools in forty-four states, the *Causal Teacher Evaluation Model* has shown that when teachers use the classroom strategies and behaviors of this model, typical student performance is increased. Greater gains can be achieved if specific strategies are used in specific ways.

Professional learning services for the *Causal Teacher Evaluation Model* include multiple-day workshops, online studies, study groups, and multiple-year commitments. These professional learning opportunities are directed at teachers, teacher leaders, instructional coaches, and school leaders.

In the 1980s, Kim Marshall, an educator from the Boston Public Schools, began to look at supervision and evaluation in new ways. In 2009, he published *Teacher Supervision and Evaluation: How to Work Smart, Build Collaboration, and Close the Achievement Gap*. This book was updated in a second edition published in 2013. There are four components to his model of supervision and evaluation.

The first component is *Mini-Observations*. Marshall developed this focus based on the weaknesses of the traditional evaluation system that required announced visits once or twice a year. He claimed that these were not accurate pictures of how teachers are doing on a daily basis. Instead, he insists on ten (about one a month) visits that are unannounced and between five and fifteen minutes depending on the purpose.

When observing classes, the Marshall model asserts that five elements are essential to good teaching and these are what the supervisor should look for. Safety is important so that the class can run smoothly. Objectives give direction to where the lesson is going. Teaching skills are the techniques that teachers use to enhance learning. Engagement means that students are paying attention and involved. Learning means that what is being taught is growth in student knowledge and skills. The Marshall model refers to these elements as *SOTEL* (Safety, Objectives, Teaching, Engagement, and Learning).

Following the unannounced observations, principals are to write a short note about what they saw. After this, principals are to deliver feedback, face-to-face, with teachers in a short exchange. Finally, the mini-observations should lead to professional learning for individual teachers and the faculty at large.

The second component is *Curriculum Planning* in which there are four elements to consider. The Marshall model asserts that each teacher should be clear about the year-end learning expectations, the first element. This involves identifying the most important standards that students in each grade and in each subject area need to learn by the end of the year.

A second element in curriculum planning is to have a curriculum calendar so that teachers know what they do week by week and month by month. The third element of curriculum planning is for teachers to plan their "backwards-designed units." By starting with learning goals and results, this can improve student achievement.

A fourth element of curriculum planning is for teachers to have good lesson plans. Rather than inspecting lesson plans, principals need to help teachers create good lesson plans that increase student achievement. As principals become involved in the knowledge of curriculum, instruction, and assessment, their mini-observations will become more meaningful and effective. Principals know what teachers are doing and what is expected of students.

The third component of the Marshall model is *Interim Assessments*. The focus here is on student learning. Most traditional teacher evaluations look at what teachers do. The Marshall model addresses student learning by inviting teachers to stop and look at student interim assessments at key moments in the semester.

Instead of doing "teach-test-move on," teachers need to analyze where students are and follow up with students not meeting the mastery levels and provide enrichment for students exceeding mastery levels. Candid data meetings can identify successes of students and areas in need of improvement. These meetings also can help teachers to plan the next steps for increasing student learning. These interim assessments are often referred to as formative assessments. The quick "on-the-spot" assessments are ways for teachers to check for understanding while teaching. Whiteboards, exit slips, and think-pair-share are ways to do this check for understanding.

The fourth component of the Marshall model is *Teacher Evaluation Rubrics*. The Marshall model identifies the most important aspects of teaching in six domains. They are Planning and Preparation for Learning; Classroom Management; Delivery of Instruction; Monitoring, Assessment, and Follow-Up; Family and Community Outreach; and Professional Responsibilities.

The Marshall model describes four levels of proficiency: highly effective, effective, improvement necessary, and does not meet standards. The rubrics are summative with the end-of-the year evaluations. For the domains and the levels of proficiency, school leaders and teachers need to have a thorough understanding of what each of these terms means in theory and practice. These domains and levels should be presented in intensive training opportunities so that teachers know what is expected of them and what defines effective teaching.

The rubrics do not assess student learning. In the Marshall model, teacher evaluation is not the way to hold teachers accountable for student learning. Instead, student learning is enhanced through the other components of the model such as mini-observations, curriculum planning, and interim assessments.

The Marshall model includes a set of ten principles that improve time management so that a principal can focus on the important things. These ten priorities are student achievement, clarify expectations, plan systematically, insist on team meetings, don't lose it, delegate effectively, observe the work, administer that ounce of prevention, get a life, and keep improving.

The Marshall model adds a few dimensions not addressed in the *Framework for Teaching* or the *Causal Teacher Evaluation* models. First, there are more teacher observations in the Marshall model than in the other models. Marshall expects supervisors to observe classrooms at least ten times per year.

Second, there was a focus on curriculum planning in collaboration with teachers. When a supervisor visited a classroom, it was already documented and everyone knew what should be taught. Third, teachers in the Marshall system were required to do more formative assessments to check for understanding versus summative assessments. Table 2.2 outlines a comparison of the three models of teacher evaluation.

As states and districts respond to the need for change, these three models of teacher evaluation emerge as possible alternatives to be adapted and used in schools. Some states have developed state-initiated plans or have modified existing models like those outlined here. Each model has the primary purpose of ensuring quality teaching and increased student learning.

Table 2.2. Comparison of Models of Teacher Evaluation

Elements	Danielson Framework for Teaching	Marzano Causal Teacher Evaluation Model	Marshall Model
Domains	1) Planning and preparation 2) The classroom environment 3) Instruction 4) Professional responsibilities	1) Classroom strategies 2) Planning and preparing 3) Reflecting on teaching 4) Collegiality and professionalism	1) Planning and preparation for learning 2) Classroom management 3) Delivery of instruction 4) Monitoring, assessment and follow-up 5) Family and community outreach 6) Professional responsibilities
Components/ elements	22 Components and 76 elements	60 Elements	4 Components
Levels of performance	1) Unsatisfactory 2) Basic 3) Proficient 4) Distinguished	1) Not using 2) Beginning 3) Developing 4) Applying 5) Innovating	1) Does not meet standards 2) Improvement necessary 3) Effective 4) Highly effective
Focus	The complexity of teaching	Use of key strategies to increase student learning	Mini-observations, curriculum planning, interim assessments, and rubrics
Professional learning	Ongoing through face-to-face, online, and research	Intensive practice based on multiple observations	Collaboration based on fourfold focus
Special features	3 Tracks: Novice and experienced teachers needing help	Deliberate practice	Time management for principals

Source: Based on an interpretation of Danielson, Marzano, Marshall models.

AN EVALUATION MODEL BASED ON PROFESSIONAL LEARNING

In addition to the models of evaluation, a *Teacher Evaluation Model for Professional Learning and Growth* has been developed (see Table 2.3). This framework uses the following domains: domain one—*designing effective instruction*, domain two—*creating a learning and growth classroom environment*, domain three—*identifying effective instructional strategies*, and domain four—*developing professional learning and growth communities*.

In domain one, the focus is on *designing effective instruction*. Effective teachers need to prepare units of instruction with clear learning outcomes (what the students should know and be able to do at the end of a unit). The instruction should be based on Common Core Standards and local district core curriculum guidelines and policies. The growth and learning outcomes are based on knowledge, reasoning, performance, and product targets.

Knowledge targets are the key understandings students need to know. Reasoning targets are how students apply these understandings. *Performance targets* are what students should be able to do. *Product targets* are what students should be able to create. These targets are the assessments that effective teachers need to include in unit plans. Students should be able to say, "I can . . ." statements. To get students to the desired outcomes and targets, effective teachers need to consider various teaching strategies. Some strategies will work with some students but not with others; therefore, instruction needs to be differentiated.

Domain two is *creating a learning and growth classroom environment*. In the first few days of school, effective teachers work collaboratively with students to establish healthy relationships, design rules, develop

Table 2.3.   Teacher Evaluation Model for Professional Learning and Growth

Elements	Model
Domains	1) Designing effective instruction based on targets
	2) Creating a growth and learning classroom environment
	3) Identifying effective instructional strategies that promote growth and learning
	4) Developing professional growth and learning communities
Components	12 Elements
Levels of performance	1) Inadequate
	2) Average
	3) Skilled
	4) Outstanding
Focus	Ongoing growth and learning for teachers, students, and school leaders

consequences, and set high expectations with clearly defined procedures for a productive learning environment. Without this positive culture and climate, learning can be compromised.

Domain three is *identifying the effective instructional strategies* that promote learning and growth for teachers and students. This is why the work of effective supervisors and evaluators is so important. A supervisor works with teachers to coach and mentor them so that they can self-evaluate. Effective teachers will come to understand their strengths and areas in need of improvement. In this ongoing process, effective teachers will develop an individual professional and learning growth plan that helps them to grow professionally as well as increases student learning and performance.

Domain four is *developing professional learning and growth communities*. For many schools, this is the ongoing development of professional learning communities where collaboration, collegiality, professionalism, communication, inquiry, and a shared focus on student learning are the priorities. Teacher leaders express this best.

Observation of teachers will be monthly walk-throughs as part of formative supervision and evaluation. Summative evaluation will depend on teacher expertise and experience. Also, state laws and union contracts also will need to be considered.

Four levels of performance, based on evidence of what is seen and heard, will guide the summative evaluations. An *inadequate* performance rating means that the teacher does not have discipline and is unable to teach the students. An *average* performance rating means that there is some teaching going on but the teacher needs improvement. A *skilled* performance rating asserts that this teacher and the students are engaged and learning. An *outstanding* performance rating means that this teacher is highly effective. Student learning and performance are excelling.

FACTORS TO CONSIDER IN CHOOSING AN EVALUATION MODEL

For local districts deciding which model to choose and adapt, several factors need to be considered. First, a committee of teachers, principals, district human resources, and union representatives needs to be formed and meet regularly to consider all the options available. The committee needs to research possible models of teacher evaluation and discuss these findings to determine the advantages and disadvantages of each model. This committee needs to review past evaluation systems for their strengths and weaknesses. Most important, the committee needs to identify the current learning needs of students and instructional growth areas for teachers.

Other issues to consider include initial administrator and teacher training with follow-up training. Technology and communication needs also must be considered. Ongoing professional learning must be a priority to meet the needs of teachers and administrators so that everyone is onboard with the new teacher evaluation system. A common language needs to be developed so that everyone understands the system.

Once this happens, a decision needs to be made and a model selected for the district. This may be adopting or modifying an existing model or creating a district stand-alone model. Budget concerns need to be addressed in this process so that the costs are identified. Those costs include planning, creating, training, implementing, and evaluating a new teacher evaluation system.

SUMMARY

Federal initiatives have pushed educators to be more accountable about the quality of teaching with the outcome of increased student learning and performance. ESEA, NCLB, and RTTT are three examples of this. The InTASC standards have become the groundwork for professional teacher standards for many states. The NBPTS have also added to teachers becoming certified at the national level. ISLLC and ELCC standards have provided a vision for school leaders to improve teacher supervision and evaluation that lead to professional learning with an effect upon student growth.

Three models of teacher evaluation have emerged that respond to the needs of school districts, schools, and teachers. The *Framework for Teaching* model gives schools a description of the complexity of teaching and learning. The *Causal Teacher Evaluation Model* focuses on teaching strategies that increase student learning and teacher expertise. The *Marshall model* highlights the importance of multiple observations aided by curriculum development, formative assessments, and rubrics.

Another model, the *Teacher Evaluation Model for Professional Learning and Growth*, was presented, which combines the features of the Danielson, Marzano, and Marshall models in an integrative manner. All four models point to the importance of supervision, evaluation, and professional learning so that student learning increases at a high proficiency level.

> gives a standard expectation for how to do this

CASE STUDY

You have been elected by the members of the faculty to be the representative on the district team that will create, implement, and evaluate the new teacher evaluation system for the district. Based on the readings from this chapter, develop a list of questions and concerns you will bring to the district team about the evaluation system.

EXERCISES AND DISCUSSION QUESTIONS

1. How do ESEA, NCLB, and RTTT affect your teaching experiences?
2. How would you design your responses to the NBPTS application to be a nationally certified teacher? Be sure to read over the Five Propositions of Accomplished Teaching.
3. Use your state professional standards of teaching to create a professional development plan for yourself.
4. What are the strengths and weaknesses of the *Framework for Teaching*, the *Causal Teacher Evaluation Model*, and the Marshall model of teacher evaluation?
5. Evaluate how your school district adapted, created, and implemented a new teacher evaluation model that meets the needs of your teachers.

REFERENCES

American Recovery and Reinvestment Act. (2009). https://www.govtrack.us/congress/bills/111/hr1

California Teaching Performance Expectations. (2013). http://www.ctc.ca.gov/educator-prep/standards/adopted-TPEs-2013.pdf

Council for the Accreditation of Educator Preparation (CAEP). (2012). http://www.caep@caepnet.org

Council of Chief State School Officers. (2013). *Model core teaching standards and learning progressions for teachers 1.0: A resource for ongoing teacher development.* Washington, DC: Interstate Teacher Assessment and Support Consortium.

Danielson, C. (2007). *Enhancing professional practice: A framework for teaching* (2nd ed.). Alexandria, VA: Association for Supervision and Curriculum Development.

Danielson, C. (2010). Evaluations that help teachers learn. *Educational Leadership,* 68(4), 35–39.

Danielson, C. (2012). Observing classroom practice. *Educational Leadership, 70*(3), 32–37.

Danielson, C., and McGreal, T. (2000). *Teacher evaluation to enhance professional practice*. Alexandria, VA: Association for Supervision and Curriculum Development.

Educational Leadership Consortium Council. (2011). ELCC standards. Washington, DC: National Policy Board for Educational Administration.

Illinois Professional Teaching Standards (2013). Retrieved from http://www.isbe.state.il.us/PEAC/pdf/IL_prof_teaching_stds.pdf

Interstate School Leaders Licensure Consortium. (2011). ISLLC standards. Washington DC: Interstate School Leaders Licensure Consortium of Chief State School Officers.

Marshall, K. (2013). *Rethinking teacher supervision and evaluation* (2nd ed). San Francisco, CA: Jossey-Bass.

Marzano, R., & Toth, M. (2013). *Teacher evaluation that makes a difference: A new model for teacher growth and student achievement*. Alexandria, VA: Association for Supervision and Curriculum Development.

National Board for Professional Teaching Standards (NBPTS). (1989). *What teachers should know and be able to do*. Arlington, VA: National Board for Professional Teaching.

New York Teaching Standards. (2012). https://www.engageny.org/resource/new-york-state-teaching-standards

No Child Left Behind (NCLB) Act. (2001). Pub. L. No. 107-110, § 115, Stat. 1425 (2002).

Ohio Teacher Evaluation System. (2011). http://www.education.ohio.gov

Performance Evaluation Reform Act. (PERA). (2010). http://www.isbe.net/pera/

Race to the Top (RTTT) Act of 2011. (2011). https://www.govtrack.us/congress/bills/112/hr1532

3

✛

Professional Learning and Growth for Teacher Improvement

OBJECTIVES

At the conclusion of this chapter you will be able to:

1. Understand the importance of professional learning and growth as major factors in improving teacher effectiveness (ELCC 2, 3, 5, 6; ISLCC 2, 3, 5, 6; TLEC 1, 2, 3, 4, 5; InTASC 2, 3, 7; Learning Forward Standards).
2. Describe the similarities and differences between professional development, professional learning, professional growth, and in-service training (ELCC 2, 6; ISLCC 2, 3, 5, 6; TLEC 1, 2, 3, 4, 5; InTASC 2, 3, 7; Learning Forward Standards).
3. Recognize that evaluation and supervision are different processes but are interrelated and complement one another (ELCC 1, 2, 3, 5, 6; ISLCC 1, 2, 3, 5, 6; TLEC 1, 2, 3, 4, 5; InTASC 2, 3, 7; Learning Forward Standards).
4. Describe the relationship between supervision and professional learning and growth (ELCC 1, 2, 3, 5, 6; ISLCC 2, 3, 5, 6; TLEC 2, 3, 4, 5; InTASC 2, 3, 7; Learning Forward Standards).
5. Describe the relationship between evaluation and professional learning and growth (ELCC 1, 2, 3, 5, 6; ISLCC 1, 2, 3, 5, 6; TLEC 1, 2, 3, 4, 5; InTASC 2, 3, 7; Learning Forward Standards).

TEACHER PROFESSIONAL DEVELOPMENT

In the *Many Faces of Leadership*, Charlotte Danielson (2007) called teaching *a flat profession*. She suggested that in most professions, the more knowledge and expertise one gains, the more responsibility one assumes. However, Danielson states that in teaching, "the 20-year veteran's responsibilities are essentially the same as those of the newly licensed novice" (p. 14). The needs of teachers regarding their own *professional learning and growth* are not flat. Also, the needs of a novice teacher are far different than those of the veteran teacher. In fact, all teachers have different needs as they examine their own professional growth.

Novice teachers need more intensive support and more frequent feedback to grow into highly effective practitioners than many evaluation systems are designed to provide. The reality is that even the best-trained teachers need time and assistance to apply their knowledge and skills to their individual schools and classrooms.

If evaluation is truly the centerpiece of a performance management and professional development system that meets the needs of teachers, it needs to be paired with the structured support and ongoing, data-driven feedback that comprehensive supervision and evaluation programs should provide. Too often *professional development* activities are structured to one size fits all.

Most school districts use only a small portion of their budget for professional development. Also, the time allotted for such professional development is limited by the number of days allotted in the school calendar. It appears that school districts are not investing in the most important part of personnel management—that of ongoing, sustained training and growth for the important human resources supporting the district schools.

The use of the terms *professional development, professional learning, professional growth, staff training,* and *in-service training* often appears interchangeable. However, these terms are different in many ways. The *in-service activities* and *staff training* used by school districts are usually a one-shot, focused training on topics required by all staff and faculty, such as blood-borne pathogens, new textbook adoptions, behavior code changes, or program updates (Figure 3.1).

Professional growth and professional learning are used by teachers and administrators in planning continual opportunities for the teacher to grow in pedagogical techniques, knowledge, and content skills. This type of growth is teacher driven and geared directly to the individual needs of that teacher. These activities usually appear in the individual teacher supervision and evaluation plan (Figure 3.2).

In-Service Activities

- Blood-borne pathogens
- Behavior code changes
- Classroom management
- Common Core
- CPR
- Faculty handbook updates
- Instructional technology use
- RtI
- Textbook adoptions

Figure 3.1.   Common Types of In-Service Training

- Active teacher and supervisor collaboration
- Research and evidence based
- Driven by measureable goals
- Contains a mutually agreed upon action plan
- Includes a manageable time line
- Resources are listed and reviewed
- Evidence is collected and analyzed
- Builds content knowledge and skills
- Includes best instructional strategies and practices
- Impacts classroom instruction
- Improves teacher and student performance

Figure 3.2.   Elements of a Professional Learning and Growth Plan

Professional development is a broader, more encompassing term used by administrators and teachers to characterize multiple training and development programs within a school district and school setting. Most often all activities related to staff and faculty growth and training come under the heading of the school or district professional development plan.

As best-practice strategies for teaching continue to emerge in the research, the standards-based movement and the licensing of educators has helped to develop recommendations for teacher preparation programs and the evaluation of teachers. What began in the 1920s and continued into the late 1950s as a simple evaluation checklist with descriptions of the behaviors and functions required of classroom teachers has now become a much more complex supervisory evaluative process.

Those studying teacher behaviors in effective classrooms have identified that teaching is more than writing on a chalkboard or simply making assignments. Effective teaching requires a teacher to possess a sophisticated set of content knowledge and skills as well as a deep understanding of the learning process in children and young adults in order to impact student learning.

A cutting-edge study to first tackle the questions of what works in a large-scale, systematic way was *Mid-Continent Research for Education and Learning* (McREL), which conducted a meta-analysis of decades of studies of teacher classroom practice, selecting the most rigorous from an initial sampling of 4,000 such studies. McREL's researchers mathematically determined the most effective practices found to have a statistically significant effect on student learning measured by standardized test scores.

First published in 2001, this study, described in *Classroom Instruction That Works* (Marzano et al., 2001) changed teaching by linking classroom strategies to evidence of increased student learning. The work clearly identified successful approaches that mark effective classroom instruction. The basic premise of the study was to show that schools that use research to guide instructional practices outperform those that do not.

In a companion book, *What Works in Schools*, Robert Marzano (2003) describes eleven research-based factors shown in another large-scale research project at McREL to be essential for the larger context of an effective school. The study was a follow-up of the one done in 2001 and verified once again that teacher effectiveness is of high importance. The study was categorized into three areas of *school, teacher, and student factors*.

The *school factors* were a guaranteed and viable curriculum, challenging goals and effective feedback, parent and community involvement, a safe and orderly environment, and collegiality and professionalism. The *teacher factors* were instructional strategies, classroom management, and effective curriculum design. The *student factors* were home environment, learned intelligence and background knowledge, and motivation. These eleven factors led to the conclusion that school effectiveness and teacher effectiveness are highly interrelated in how a student learns (Marzano, 2003).

In his 90-90-90 studies, Douglas Reeves (2005) showed that high-poverty schools could also be high performing. He provided examples from multiple school systems to illustrate the common characteristics of

90-90-90 schools (over 90 percent poverty, over 90 percent minorities, and yet over 90 percent achieving at high proficiency levels).

The factors identified in the studies were a strong focus on academic achievement, clear curriculum choices, frequent assessment of student progress and multiple opportunities for improvement, an emphasis on nonfiction writing, and collaborative scoring of student work, with explicit guidelines.

Reeves stressed that teacher quality and effective leadership, not demographics, are the most dominant factors in determining student success. The effective practices and policies identified in those studies are entirely consistent with the McREL findings. It is these types of studies that effective leaders can use to improve the teaching and learning in schools and guide ongoing and effective professional learning opportunities. That is why relevant professional learning and the tracking of individual teacher growth are vital to creating effective teachers.

SUPERVISION AND BUILDING TEACHER CAPACITY FOR GROWTH

Educational research has repeatedly identified *teacher effectiveness* as one of the most important factors in student learning. The work that teachers accomplish in classrooms matters, and public education's top priority should be developing teachers. As presented in chapter 1, teacher supervision and evaluation have different outcomes, yet they complement one another.

Supervision is *formative*. It provides coaching and mentoring to build teacher capacity and help guide teachers to best research for sustained personal growth. Evaluation is *summative*. It is generally described as having two primary purposes: (1) measuring teacher performance, and (2) providing individualized feedback and support to strengthen teaching.

Many teacher supervision and evaluation procedures adopted by school districts do little to affect teacher performance. Typically, teachers and administrators view teacher supervision and evaluation procedures as bureaucratic hurdles that must be cleared. They are simply one more task evaluators must accomplish. This roadblock is magnified by the fact that many teacher supervision and evaluation plans require supervisors to formally or informally visit teacher classrooms one or two times per year, depending on teacher tenure status.

It is appropriate to have discussions about how to effectively supervise and evaluate teachers so the process is relevant to them and improves their instructional practice. Teacher supervision and evaluation are guided by two major points: (1) school leadership is central to effective teacher supervision and evaluation, and (2) teacher supervision and evaluation should be comprehensive in scope.

First, effective teacher supervision and evaluation starts with school leadership. Both district and school leaders are essential to ensure that teacher supervision and evaluation is meaningful. District leadership must adopt comprehensive and fair teacher supervision and evaluation policies and practices. Moreover, district leaders must expect and hold school leaders accountable for being in teacher classrooms daily and weekly.

This includes the central belief that district leaders are responsible for training and monitoring evaluators in how to ensure teachers are providing high-quality instruction. Effective supervisors routinely visit teacher classrooms and provide formative, relevant, and appropriate feedback to teachers. Routinely visiting classrooms is critical.

How can we create a clear picture of teacher effectiveness unless we formally and informally visit classrooms multiple times per year? Supervisors must be in all teacher classrooms weekly, for extended periods of time, and district leaders must hold them accountable for performing this task. If teacher development and personal growth is a priority, then both district and school leaders will find a way to routinely visit teacher classrooms.

Second, school districts must operationally define *effective teaching* and be clear about how to measure it. The recent trend of using only test data as the standard for teacher effectiveness is flawed. Teaching is a social endeavor having many complex variables that affect student learning, and teachers are the most significant. Student test scores should be used as one piece of data in a comprehensive supervision and evaluation model. Data collected may come from such varied sources as:

- classroom observations (assessed by principals, teacher leaders, instructional coaches, or peers);
- student assessment data on various indicators focused on growth (mostly formative assessments);
- instructional artifacts like student work, scoring rubrics, and lesson plans;
- teacher self-reflection within journals or logs;
- age-appropriate student or parent surveys; and
- teacher-developed professional development and growth plans.

One key in selecting data sources is to ensure teachers have buy-in regarding what they perceive as fair and representative of *quality teaching*. But supervisors should also have non-negotiables in the process. These non-negotiables may include such areas as:

- posting daily classroom instructional schedules that are visible to students;
- clearly identifying and posting essential learning standards in "student-friendly" language;
- developing, implementing, and posting a classroom behavior plan that supports and aligns with the school-wide behavior code; and
- providing ongoing opportunities for students to achieve subject matter mastery.

There may be other non-negotiables as determined by the school and district environment in which the teachers work. Supervisors must solicit teacher feedback about teacher performance expectations in the supervisory process if they expect the procedures to affect day-to-day classroom practice.

When school leaders wear the supervisory hat, they are *coaching, mentoring, collaborating,* and *actively assisting* teachers in the classroom. They become another set of eyes and ears in that classroom to improve and monitor student learning. The school leader creates opportunities for collaborative dialogue to discuss classroom management, instructional methodology, current research, and student learning goals.

The supervisory hat permits the school leader to be a mentor and to guide the teacher to relevant and effective research in best practices. Together the school leader and teacher can develop relevant goals for teacher growth that directly affect the day-to-day learning of students.

Generally speaking, all teachers can benefit from good coaching and mentoring. Mentoring can help teachers when faced with issues in dealing with disruptive students, personal problems that affect teaching, administrative requirements, and clarifying the responsibilities of the position. School leaders should be well trained in how to be effective supervisors in the mentoring and coaching process.

In supervision, the relationship between supervisor and teacher is critical to success in teacher growth. Topics for coaching and mentoring may include understanding instruction and curriculum, managing student discipline, understanding the school district operations, and reviewing district policies and procedures. In addition to these professional qualities, a mentor needs effective coaching skills, which include being personal, sensitive, and understanding; establishing rapport; and giving constructive feedback (Tomal et al., 2014).

Finally, it should be noted that the summative evaluation process is simply an analysis of data collected during the supervision process. Sustained teacher supervision is the only way to improve teacher instructional practice. Educational resources need to be devoted to the improvement of teaching practices rather than simply be used to assign a label to teacher performance. What then is the necessary role of evaluation in the supervision and evaluation process?

Effective Supervision

- Active coaching and mentoring
- Mutual collaboration and sharing of ideas
- Provides constructive feedback
- Multiple classroom visits (informal and formal)
- Active counseling and monitoring by supervisor
- Conflict mediation when needed
- Measureable and relevant goals
- Monitors, records, and analyzes the outcomes

Figure 3.3. Qualities of an Effective Supervision Plan

EVALUATION AND BUILDING TEACHER CAPACITY FOR GROWTH

Like students, teachers are also learners. The best way to improve student learning is to strengthen the instructional practices of teachers through job-embedded professional learning and instructional support. Evaluation systems have a critical role to play in informing this work, and the ones conceived with this in mind will be most likely to succeed.

Teacher evaluation must focus more on the act of teaching. Policies and procedures must not only measure teacher performance but also provide pathways to develop and improve teaching practice. A well-designed *teacher evaluation plan* might better be termed a *performance management plan*. Its primary purposes must be to maximize the act of teaching and to improve delivery of instruction.

A critical component of an aligned district-wide process is teacher evaluation. It provides embedded opportunities for teachers to continually learn and grow. Evaluation is also most effective when it is integrated with other processes that support professional learning and growth.

Teacher evaluation needs to provide individual teachers with the opportunity (1) to analyze the process, (2) determine the effect on their instruction, and (3) make modifications based on that analysis. What teachers need is less of the performance ratings and more of the data-driven feedback on their practice. A commitment to educator ongoing learning, including the creation of personalized professional learning plans, should be a central focus in a comprehensive evaluation process.

These plans should point teachers toward specific and highly relevant learning opportunities that allow them to address areas of instruction that need improvement. It means that evaluators must understand effective instruction. This will happen only when those responsible for evaluating, coaching, and mentoring teachers are trained in the art of providing meaningful, developmental feedback; encouraging reflection; and creating opportunities for professional learning and growth.

If designed as part of a comprehensive plan, feedback on instruction, reflection, and mentoring activities change professional development from a one-time or infrequent event to continual growth activities. It is critical that districts build these principles and structures into their evaluation processes because a systemic teacher evaluation plan will succeed or fail based on its ability to improve teaching and ultimately student learning (Figure 3.4).

The models or frameworks used for evaluation of teachers must be research based. What is important is that the evaluators and the teachers need to agree upon the model and the process that will be used, have a shared language, and have a common understanding and definition of what the elements of effective teaching are.

A meaningful evaluation process transitions directly from a relevant supervisory process. An honest evaluation with reliable and constructive feedback based on evidence without bias will enable teachers to continue to

Effective Evaluation

- Provides developmental and meaningful feedback
- Research and outcome based
- Driven by measureable goals
- Encourages active teacher reflection
- Creates opportunities for continuing growth
- Focuses on building content knowledge
- Focuses on building instructional methodology
- Directly impacts teacher and student performance
- Provides a rating of teacher performance

Figure 3.4.   **Qualities of an Effective Evaluation Plan**

learn and grow. Both are based on developing a collaborative and trusting coaching and mentoring relationship between the teacher and the evaluator.

When school leaders wear the evaluator's hat, they gather evidence and data from multiple sources and make judgments about teacher performance. These sources may include student surveys, classroom observations, classroom drop-ins, and student achievement results gleaned from standardized summative and formative district and grade level assessments. All of the data gathered must be analyzed by teachers and the school leader to identify teacher professional growth needs. One comprehensive way to conduct this analysis is through the Danielson framework.

The Danielson framework (Danielson, 2007), reviewed in chapter 2, divides teaching into four domains: (1) Planning and Preparation, (2) Classroom Environment, (3) Instruction, and (4) Professional Responsibilities. The framework domains have twenty-two components and seventy-six elements. The framework also allows teachers to be rated at four performance levels: distinguished, proficient, basic, and unsatisfactory. Such tools and rubrics like those in the Danielson framework can successfully measure teacher effectiveness and provide teachers with relevant feedback on the factors that matter for improving student learning.

School districts can create alignment between evaluator priorities and coaching priorities by using the Danielson framework to guide individual teacher evaluation, self-assessment, and mentoring. This necessitates a system of open communication between teachers and evaluators. It also requires a shared protocol (common language) for assessing teaching within the district supervision and evaluation process.

RESEARCH-BASED SUPERVISION AND EVALUATION

By enhancing and building upon the "clinical supervision" model, we can use it as a tool for change and teacher growth that results in more effective teaching and increased student achievement. The traditional evaluation process based on the clinical supervision model has usually been a one-way progression, which will be further presented and discussed in chapter 6. However, this process has typically consisted of the following steps:

1. *Written notification of pre-observation conference*: Teacher receives notice that an evaluation is due early in the school year. The teacher is invited to a pre-observation conference when the time and location of the observation is determined.
2. *Pre-observation conference*: Conversation with teacher regarding the time and location of the observation. Teacher is asked to submit the lesson plan ahead of time with objectives listed and detailed plan.

3. *Observation*: Administrator shows up at appointed time and writes a narrative of the lesson observed.
4. *Narrative write-up*: Administrator fills out required district forms for teacher evaluation and provides copies for teacher by required contract time line.
5. *Post-observation conference*: Teacher and administrator discuss written evaluation and performance rating. Both teacher and administrator sign off as having read and discussed the written document regarding the evaluation process.
6. *Sign off with signatures*: Both parties agree that they have concluded the process required.

Unfortunately, most scheduled observations occur infrequently in this model. The quality of classroom instruction observed may not be representative of what students experience on a daily basis.

Often in school districts, there is a lack of alignment between observation and gathering hard data as evidence. There is little or no planning for professional learning and growth for the teacher in the evaluation cycle. Basically, the traditional evaluation process is a time-intensive process without much impact on teacher effectiveness or student performance. Teachers become passive recipients in the evaluation process isolated from their peers. For teachers to professionally grow in an effective evaluation process, they must be active and reflective participants.

When a research-based model is implemented, a lengthy training period is needed for both evaluators and teachers. They must become familiar with the steps in the supervisory and evaluation process. They must share knowledge and develop a common language defining effective teaching. They must develop a shared understanding of what constitutes effective instruction and the expectations of teachers in that district to meet those expectations.

It is possible that teachers who in the past have received excellent performance ratings may now receive satisfactory or needs improvement ratings. This may create an uncomfortable climate for some teachers who have received high ratings for a long time using the traditional supervision and evaluation model based on one or two classroom observations every two years and summative narratives as feedback.

Instructional leaders need to develop strategies for supporting and improving teachers throughout the implementation process. Expectations must be raised, but resources and leadership are the keys to improving teacher performance in the classroom when using a research-based evaluation plan. What is important to the evaluation and supervision of teachers is the central goal that teachers must grow in expertise to become more effective in their classrooms.

The effective school leader should establish clear and fair guidelines for the evaluation supervisory process. These may include:

- the use of a collaborative goal-setting process;
- the establishment of mutually agreed upon non-negotiables for achievement and instruction;
- a clear alignment to school improvement plans and the values, vision, mission, and goals of the district;
- a research-based data collection process that monitors and documents ongoing achievement and instructional goals; and
- the allocation of resources to support the goals for achievement and instruction in the school and district.

All of these actions must be implemented collaboratively when working with individual teachers. Guiding this process must be a clear vision and mission for the district and schools supporting the principle that every child can learn. Student performance goals should permit students multiple opportunities to demonstrate what they have learned and that they can use the knowledge and skills identified within the established district curriculum. Creative leadership is central to supporting a systemic use of the professional learning and growth supervisory evaluation process.

INDIVIDUAL PROFESSIONAL LEARNING AND GROWTH PLANS

The use of the *Standards for Professional Learning* (2011) may be one step to beginning an effective supervision and evaluation plan for teachers. The *Standards for Professional Learning* is the third iteration of standards outlining the characteristics of professional learning that lead to effective teaching practices, supportive leadership, and improved student results. Learning Forward (formerly the National Staff Development Council), with the contribution of forty professional associations and education organizations, developed the *Standards for Professional Learning*.

These standards make explicit that the purpose of professional learning is for educators to develop the knowledge, skills, practices, and dispositions they need to help students perform at higher levels. The standards are not a prescription for how education leaders and public officials should address all the challenges related to improving the performance of educators and their students. Instead, they focus on the central issue of teacher professional learning and growth.

To develop a new perspective for teacher professional learning and growth, there is a need to create a learning organization with identified learning communities at grade and content levels committed to continual

Table 3.2 Learning Forward Professional Learning Standards, 2011

Learning Communities:
Professional learning that increases educator effectiveness and results for all students occurs within learning communities committed to continual improvement, collective responsibility, and goal alignment.

Leadership:
Professional learning that increases educator effectiveness and results for all students requires skillful leaders who develop capacity, advocate, and create support systems for professional learning.

Resources:
Professional learning that increases educator effectiveness and results for all students requires prioritizing, monitoring, and coordinating resources for educator learning.

Learning Designs:
Professional learning that increases educator effectiveness and results for all students integrates theories, research, and models of human learning to achieve its intended outcomes.

Implementation:
Professional learning that increases educator effectiveness and results for all students applies research on change and sustains support for implementation of professional learning for long-term change.

Outcomes:
Professional learning that increases educator effectiveness and results for all students aligns its outcomes with educator performance and student curriculum standards.

---

improvement, collective responsibility, and goal alignment. Allotting time and resources for collaboration by these groups on a regular basis during the school day, months, and year is a requirement. In addition, training in team skills will assist with the transformation of the culture and climate of the individual, group, and organization.

Supervisors and evaluators must act as instructional leaders who can articulate the overall vision and mission of the district regarding the goal that all students must have the opportunity to master the knowledge and skills identified in an articulated curriculum that is aligned with national and state standards. Finally, there is a fundamental need for teachers and students to be lifelong learners with continual individual, group, and organizational improvement as the underlying foundation of the district as a learning community.

Even though each teacher is looked upon as a lifelong learner in a professional learning community, it is important to differentiate the need for and the quantity of supervision and evaluation of teachers. Teachers who receive performance ratings of *distinguished, exceeding,* or *excellent* may not need to be evaluated every year. Teachers who receive performance ratings of *meet* or *proficient* may need to be evaluated every other year and encouraged to continue to grow so that they enhance teaching pedagogy.

However, novice teachers who need much coaching and mentoring and those veteran teachers who receive ratings of *unsatisfactory* or *needs improvement* must be monitored more closely on an annual basis. If their status remains unchanged, consideration should be given to dismissal because they may not have the ability to grow or improve or they are choosing not to grow professionally. Addressing the needs of the unsatisfactory and *marginal teacher* is discussed in chapter 6 under remediation plans.

When teachers are ineffective in the classroom, they affect student performance in a profoundly negative way. It is unfair to the students assigned to an ineffective or marginal teacher because they may not have the same opportunities to perform as do their peers who have been assigned to a more effective teacher. Field research has clearly documented that effective classroom practices result in higher performing learners.

Evaluators need to have the moral courage to deal with unsatisfactory and marginal teachers. It is an unpleasant task but one that needs to be carried through if we are following a vision of a learning organization with all members of the organization being lifelong learners who continue to learn and grow together. True instructional leaders will ensure that every child is receiving an equal opportunity to learn with an effective teacher.

In this environment, teachers will be expected to continue to learn, improve, and become more effective teachers. The expectations are set by the norms of the learning organization and its collective members. This will have a profound effect on the entire district and schools as each teacher becomes more effective no matter his or her performance level. It is possible that the whole professional learning organization will collectively and individually demonstrate improvement, which will positively affect the learning goals and performance levels of the students served by the organization.

In the research-based environment, accountability and more supervisory "hands-on" guidance and coaching are required. As an *instructional leader*, the school and district leaders are out in classrooms a majority of their time. In addition, effective leaders will use the talent and expertise of identified effective teachers to coach and mentor those peers who are given a rating of unsatisfactory or needs improvement to help improve teacher effectiveness.

School and district leaders who are planning for teacher growth must develop capacity, advocate, and create support systems for professional learning. They must prioritize, monitor, and coordinate resources and make them available for each teacher. Multiple forms and sources of data should be used to identify teacher needs, and to plan, assess, and evaluate professional learning (see Figure 3.2).

The application of research on change and professional learning should be applied with sustained support during implementation until long-term change is embedded in the culture of the organization. The evaluation process should be an outgrowth of the supervisory process.

The outcomes should align with national and state standards, content standards, district vision and mission, school improvement plans, and, most important, the expected learning goals of the district. The ultimate goals must always be improved student performance and teacher continuing growth.

SUMMARY

Researchers have conducted a meta-analysis of studies focused on teacher effectiveness. An analysis of the research data has indicated that effective teaching is one of the most important variables directly affecting student performance. All children deserve to have an effective teacher in their classroom.

Research and field practice have defined what elements comprise relevant and effective professional development plans. Such district and school plans must contain multiple development and training opportunities. The activities must target individual teacher professional learning and growth based on the needs of the teacher and the level of experience and background she or he has had in the classroom setting.

How do we support and encourage teachers to become more effective in what they do? An answer is in a research-based and comprehensive evaluation and supervision plan focused on individual teacher needs. This requires that school and district leaders act as effective evaluators and supervisors. They must be in classrooms on a regular basis, provide immediate and reliable feedback about what was observed, and provide constructive suggestions for growth.

At the same time, an improved formal evaluation process must emerge that will require school and district leaders to use information gathered from multiple sources such as walk-throughs, student surveys, and other methods of gathering data over time. This enhanced process allows the evaluator to become more informed about the teacher's performance, the climate, and the culture of the classroom. Effective supervision and evaluation must reflect a true picture of the daily life of a teacher and the students in that classroom.

Using all of the data collected, the teacher and evaluator can identify professional needs and develop an individual professional learning and growth plan with goals, action steps, a time line, the person(s) responsible, resources, and evidence of completion. All teachers will have a professional learning and growth plan. Everyone will be considered a lifelong learner and an active participant in the professional learning community with the goal of becoming a more effective and skilled teacher.

CASE STUDY

You have been appointed as the new principal of Oak Woods Middle School. In your induction with the superintendent, supervision and evaluation of faculty was extensively discussed. Your district recently added professional learning and growth plans to the district board, and the union approved a supervision and evaluation process that includes final performance ratings of excellent, satisfactory, needs improvement, and unsatisfactory.

Your superintendent brought to your attention that two non-tenured teachers will become eligible for tenure at the conclusion of this academic year. He suggested you review past evaluations and performance outcomes very closely before making your recommendations to him and the board for renewal and tenure.

As you reviewed the past evaluations from the previously retired principal, you discover that both teachers were reviewed once each year for the past three years with only two classroom observations per year. Non-tenure teacher #1 is a mathematics teacher, and it appears from the previous evaluations that she is having difficulties in three areas: weak classroom management, weak content knowledge, and poor interactions with colleagues. She has received a performance rating of satisfactory in all three years of her evaluations.

Non-tenure teacher #2 is a language arts teacher and appears to be loved by students, parents, and colleagues. His classroom is "center based" and appears to actively engage the middle level learner. He is an effective user of technology in the classroom and embraces it in his classroom using student laptops and handheld devices to support and enrich classroom instruction.

Yet, he seems to have stepped outside the approved district reading and language arts curriculum and will not use the reading textbook or the ancillary materials purchased by the district for classroom use. Instead, he insists on creating what he terms are his own "authentic learning materials" for his students. He has received a performance rating of excellent in all three years of his evaluations.

Because your district has added professional learning and growth plans to the supervisory and evaluation process, develop and write an action plan for each non-tenure teacher that will provide a fair, evidence-based, and collaborative approach for the supervision and evaluation process during this academic year.

What components would each professional learning plan contain for each teacher? What supervisory steps will you take to mentor and coach these two teachers? What evidence will you determine is needed so that a fair and accurate appraisal is given about these two teachers and their classroom instructional skills and knowledge?

EXERCISES AND DISCUSSION QUESTIONS

1. What steps are needed for establishing positive relationships in the supervisory role?
2. Research the skills and dispositions involved in coaching and mentoring. What are the differences and what are the similarities?
3. What is the difference between evaluation and supervision? Can an instructional leader wear both hats at the same time? If so, how?
4. Why is it important for a district to select a framework for teaching that can be used by all teachers, evaluators, and supervisors? How does this framework help teachers to become more effective? What kind of professional development would you provide for your teachers so that they would become familiar with the framework and recognize effective teaching?
5. How does the professional learning and growth supervision and evaluation process differ from the traditional teacher evaluation process? How may this process increase student performance?
6. Develop a professional learning and growth plan for yourself based on your identified needs and professional goals. Develop a plan that includes the following: measureable goals, action steps, a time line, resources, the person(s) responsible, and evidence submitted, and how it affects and is applied in your classroom.

REFERENCES

Danielson, C. (2007). *Enhancing professional practice: A framework for teaching*. (2nd ed.). Alexandria, VA: Association for Supervision and Curriculum Development.

Danielson, C. (2007). The many faces of leadership. *Educational Leadership, 65*(1), 14–19.

Marzano, R. (2003). *What works in schools: Translating research into action.* Alexandria, VA: Association for Supervision and Curriculum Development.

Marzano, R., Pickering, D., & Pollock, J. (2001). *Classroom instruction that works: Research-based strategies for increasing student achievement.* Alexandria, VA: Association for Supervision and Curriculum Development.

Reeves, D. (2005). *Accountability in action: A blueprint for learning organizations.* (2nd ed.). Denver, CO: Advanced Learning Press.

Standards for Professional Learning. (2011). Canton, Ohio: Learning Forward.

Tomal, D., Schilling, C., & Wilhite, R. (2014). *The teacher leader: Core competencies and strategies for effective leadership.* Lanham, MD: Rowman & Littlefield Education, Inc.

4

Differentiating Professional Learning and Growth Plans

OBJECTIVES

At the conclusion of this chapter you will be able to:

1. Understand and apply the 2011 Learning Forward *Standards for Professional Learning* in the development of a professional learning community (ELCC 1, 2, 3, 5, 6; ISLLC 1, 2, 3, 5, 6; TLEC 1, 2, 3, 4, 5; InTASC 1, 2, 3, 4, 5; Learning Forward Standards).
2. Develop differentiated professional learning and growth plans based on the identified needs of a district, a school, and an individual (ELCC 1 2, 3, 5, 6; ISLLC 1, 2, 3, 5, 6; TLEC 1, 2, 3, 4, 5; InTASC 1, 2, 3, 4, 5; Learning Forward Standards).
3. Describe the leadership characteristics of school leaders that foster effective teaching and professional learning (ELCC 1, 2, 3, 5, 6; ISLLC 1, 2, 3, 5, 6; TLEC 1, 2, 3, 4, 5; InTASC 1, 2, 3, 4, 5; Learning Forward Standards).

STANDARDS FOR PROFESSIONAL LEARNING

A critical component in transforming schools is to include a comprehensive approach to teacher pedagogical skill improvement. Previous chapters have focused on using an effective professional learning and growth plan that is linked to an effective evaluation process for building teacher effectiveness. This chapter will focus on the Learning Forward *Standards for Professional Learning* (see chapter 3, Figure 3.5) and the differentiation of professional learning plans in a *professional learning community* (PLC).

Professional learning and growth plans should be aligned with the six Learning Forward standards. These standards have not been prioritized or numbered because they are holistic and not linear. This means that each standard is equally important in the design of professional learning and growth plans whether they are for a teacher, school, or district. The standards are focused on direct improvement in effective instructional methodology. The Learning Forward *Standards for Professional Learning* are delineated and examples are provided in the following section.

The Professional Learning Community

Learning communities focus on professional learning and growth that increases teacher effectiveness. Increased student performance levels occur within learning communities that are committed to continual improvement, collective responsibility, and goal alignment. High expectations for all students and clearly articulated goals for student achievement are the norm in learning communities.

The concept of *professional learning communities* can be traced from the early work of Peter Senge (1990). In his book *The Fifth Discipline: The Art and Practice of a Learning Organization*, five disciplines of a learning organization are outlined: (1) *personal mastery*, (2) *mental models*, (3) *building shared visions*, (4) *team learning*, and (5) *systems thinking*.

His work integrated the five disciplines into a coherent body of methods, tools, and principles for building the capacity of an organization. The system is oriented to examine the interrelatedness of the five elements and see them as part of a common process. Although his book was written for the business community, it has been used by educators in organizational theory and development.

DuFour and Eaker (1998) built on Senge's work and defined a learning organization in schools as a *professional learning community*. Adapting the five disciplines, DuFour and Eaker developed the characteristics of a professional learning community. Table 4.1 provides a conceptual linkage between Senge and the DuFour-Eaker ideas about learning organizations. Professional learning communities are built around the philosophy that the core mission of each district, school, and individual is the acknowledgment that all students can learn. Creating a shared mission and vision with defined goals is the key building block of a PLC. There are fundamental questions that provide a foundation for the work in a PLC. These are:

- What are the learning goals and objectives?

Table 4.1.   Disciplines of a Learning Organization Applied to Schools

Learning Organization	Professional Learning Community (PLC)
Systems thinking	Culture and climate that promotes collaboration and builds relationships on trust and respect.
Personal mastery	Resources and interventions that meet individual needs and encourage growth and learning.
Mental models	Values and beliefs framed around continual lifelong learning for faculty, staff, and students.
Shared vision	Vision of helping all students achieve at a high level of learning.
Team learning	Developing organizational structures and processes that provide adequate time for team learning and growth activities.

Source: Based on the works of Senge, DuFour, and Esker.

- How will these goals and objectives be evaluated?
- How will learning experiences be differentiated?
- How often and when will learning experiences be retooled or redefined?

Instructional leaders and teachers must continually address these foundational priorities. There must a clear understanding of what students need to know and be able to do. Educators need to be able to apply a variety of instructional strategies to meet individual needs. Likewise, educators need to recognize that the amount of time varies for students to master the learning objectives.

Members of PLCs should believe in continual growth for themselves and their students. Also, people need to assume responsibility for continual improvement. Their goals must be aligned with the mission of the district and school. PLC members must believe that all students can reach the *learning targets* set out for them. Authentic learning communities with well-established values and beliefs will experience continual learning and growth experiences even when they are already performing at a high level.

Effective leaders need to be aware that during the early stages of implementation, the professional learning community model can reach a critical point called the *implementation dip*, where enthusiasm begins to diminish. The professional learning community can become less focused and somewhat confused.

During this time, there is a need for school leaders to continue to articulate the vision and mission of the organization that reflect the core principles of the professional learning community. Repetition of the vision and mission statements will help to refocus the members of the PLC.

Building a professional learning community could take two to three years for the implementation to become embedded in the values and beliefs of a school and district. Change seems simple in the designed plan. However, during the implementation of the plan, the change is complex. There must be opportunities for members of the PLC to understand and incorporate the changes into a daily plan of action.

Leadership

School leaders need to have the courage, energy, and commitment to build, develop, and maintain a healthy school climate and culture. The leader's primary job is to assess and monitor the climate and culture of the school. This assessment can be accomplished by administering surveys and questionnaires, and having formal and informal conversations with stakeholders. Being in classrooms and hallways on a regular basis to observe teacher and student behavior can also provide relevant information.

Leaders should facilitate the development or revision of the vision, mission, values, and goals of the school (key school performance indicators). These should align with the district *key performance indicators*. Successful PLC leaders keep these indicators visible to all members. This is important to staying the course in meeting mutually agreed upon goals and outcomes.

For trust and respect to become embedded as strong values in the culture, a school leader must build relationships based on honesty and trust. Figure 4.1 describes some of the leadership skills for building quality relationships. The foundation of a positive culture and climate rests with treating everyone fairly and with dignity.

All people working in a school must believe that they play an important role in the education of students. They must believe that they are

- Listens with good eye contact and respectful body language,
- Respects the role of individuals and their perspective,
- Acts with integrity and is responsive,
- Creates a culture and climate that is orderly, safe, and respectful,
- Provides supervision and evaluation that fosters effective coaching, mentoring, and encourages lifelong learning,
- Matches leadership with individual's skills and talent,
- Demonstrates sincere personal regard and respect for others.

Figure 4.1.   Leadership Skills for Building Quality Relationships

respected and welcomed members of the team. They must be committed to the idea that every child can and will learn.

The school leader listens carefully and is respectful of all thoughts and ideas. The leader must know when to ask questions during a conversation with a teacher to better understand the role of the individual and the perspectives shared. Demonstrating sincere personal regard for others is a critical characteristic for a school leader.

School leaders need to be able to develop capacity, advocate for, and create support systems for professional learning. Effective and constructive coaching and mentoring are used during supervision. They should also possess the ability to match opportunity for leadership with an individual's skills and talent.

Building capacity for faculty and staff requires a school leader to be creative and to use the talent in the schools and district to support professional learning. Effective school leaders are those who focus the majority of their time on teaching and learning. They are school leaders who transform the culture and climate of their workplace.

Resources

It is important that instructional leaders prioritize, monitor, and coordinate the resources for educator learning. After assessing the needs of faculty and staff for professional learning, it is critical to prioritize the needs. Resources should be budgeted accordingly. Already available faculty and staff who have expertise and are highly effective can be called upon to mentor and coach fellow colleagues. School leaders should be encouraged to write grants that are focused on the prioritized needs for the development of quality professional learning and growth of faculty and staff.

Developing professional learning plans based on opinion or the "latest and greatest" trends without support from research and relevant data will lead to misalignment of goals. Too often districts and schools that continue to make little or no improvement in student achievement year after year have not developed learning communities or professional learning and growth plans for teachers. They continue down the same path with little regard for providing relevant learning opportunities. School leaders must be committed to monitoring and allocating resources for the development of ongoing professional learning.

Data

Professional learning opportunities that increase educator effectiveness and results for all students should be based on a variety of sources and types of data. The data analyzed by PLCs would include student, teacher, and system data. These data are used to plan, assess, and evaluate the needs for professional learning.

Every PLC team should be involved in examining and analyzing both formative and summative student data. The results of this examination can be used to establish new goals for the group, each teacher, and students. The team should continue to review the data throughout the school year for evidence of progress.

As progress is made and goals are accomplished, new goals and targets are set. Continual improvement is the priority. The whole organization continues to grow in this environment, and the continuum of expertise will continue to expand within the capacity of each teacher. All teachers and students will benefit, and performance levels should increase.

Schools often have multiple sources of data to collect and analyze. Yet teachers often do not have the training or skills to use the information available. A careful analysis of the data should enable them to set goals and define outcomes that will result in an increase in teacher effectiveness. They will begin to note student achievement increases.

When PLC team members are taught how to understand the data from varied assessments, they can identify how their students are performing across the school year. Areas of strength and areas for growth can be identified. The members of the team can reflect individually and collectively to generate new ideas or share successful strategies for teaching. Then, a professional learning and growth community has been established.

Designs

Professional learning that increases educator effectiveness integrates theories, research, and models of human learning to achieve its intended outcomes. When districts adopt new ideas and practices for teaching and learning, there must be a detailed research-based investigation. The review must focus on best instructional practices, curriculum, or resources that are proven to increase student classroom performance and enhance teaching.

Most teachers have experienced back-to-school in-service training that was designed to be entertaining but had little to do with the improvement of instruction in classrooms and was certainly not research based. It is a *feel-good experience* that does not translate to improvement of instruction in the classroom.

An individual teacher can have a significant effect on student achievement. Effective teachers set objectives and provide constructive feedback. They reinforce learning and provide recognition of student performance. Cooperative learning and differentiated instruction are the norm for the classroom. Effective teachers use research-based strategies such as cues, questions, advanced organizers, summarizing and note taking, identifying similarities and differences, or generating and testing hypotheses. They assign meaningful homework and provide guided practice and multiple opportunities for students to test knowledge and learn.

Knowing these strategies and when and how to use them is the basis of teacher effectiveness. They should be included in the learning design of lessons. Multiple strategies increase student achievement when used appropriately and at the right time during a unit or lesson. Using them randomly or out of a learning context is not always effective and has less impact on student performance. The key question is how effectively are these strategies being used?

The professional learning community model requires hard work and commitment. The focus is on learning instead of on teaching (see Figure 4.2). Colleagues working collaboratively together to reach goals will make a difference. Evaluating the outcomes and adjusting their action steps to meet those goals or setting new goals with higher levels of performance is important to increasing teacher growth and learning.

High-performing professional learning communities do not just happen. Principals and teacher leaders who are instructional leaders have to work hard to keep the group focused with the target on the outcomes. The development of measurable goals and the continual monitoring of assessment data are necessary to make sure there is strong alignment to teaching and learning.

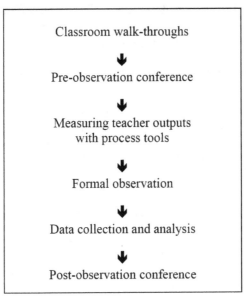

Figure 4.2. Professional Learning and Supervision Plan

Implementation

Professional learning that increases educator effectiveness and results in sustained change is the goal of effective implementation. Long-term change must have an effect on the vision, mission, values, and beliefs of the school. It must cause permanent change in the culture and climate of the school, the family, and the community.

High-quality professional learning opportunities for teachers and leaders must be embedded and sustained. This is a critical issue because research indicates that there is a high correlation between teacher effectiveness and increased student performance.

Outcomes

Professional learning that increases educator effectiveness and results for all students aligns its outcomes with educator performance and student curriculum standards. Before a school can become a professional learning community, the members must agree upon a common shared language and knowledge about what constitutes effective teaching.

Teachers and school leaders can increase effectiveness by agreeing upon the results they desire and by developing effective teaching instruction practices and demonstrating key affective domains of learning to achieve the school goals (see Table 4.2). Allowing teachers to take ownership in practicing key instructional decisions creates effective links between leadership responsibilities and the implementation process.

Adding this element of ownership for outcomes can and will bring about individual, group, and organizational learning and growth at the

Table 4.2. Effective Teacher Instruction Practices and Affective Learning Domain

Instructional	Affective
Sets expectations for students	Uses self-reflection
Gives clear directions and procedures	Sets high expectations
Explains content with creativity	Uses multiple instructional strategies
Asks questions that are high quality	Is sensitive to others
Creates genuine discussion	Is creative
Engages students	Displays enthusiasm
Sets high expectations for self and students	Is respectful
Uses formative and summative assessment	Maintains accurate record keeping
Differentiates instruction	Is responsible
Uses project-based learning	Is flexible
Uses effective instructional materials	Is respectful of others
Provides learning opportunities	Demonstrates mastery of content
Uses coherent structure and pacing	Is a servant leader
Applies content and pedagogy	Is a lifelong learner

classroom, school, and district levels. Teacher buy-in is necessary and will result in positive change in classroom strategies. Enhanced and improved teacher performance will lead to increases in student learning and enrich the professional learning community.

DIFFERENTIATING PROFESSIONAL GROWTH AND LEARNING

Differentiating professional growth and learning plans for individuals, groups, and organizations is a necessary component of supervision and evaluation. Teacher strengths and growth needs must be identified through the collection and analysis of data. Goals can then be set and action steps determined. These plans still need to be designed and guided by the elements of a professional learning and growth plan as previously outlined in chapter 3.

Most states have adopted a research-based model or framework to be used for the evaluation of teachers (review Figure 2.4 in chapter 2). Also most states have established a model for teacher evaluation. Very few states allow a district to design its own version of an evaluation system. If a district does design its own system, it must be approved and have alignment with the state-established evaluation guidelines.

Before any framework is implemented in a school or district, a training period is needed for evaluators, supervisors, and teachers. It is important that they become familiar with the process and procedures of the evaluation model or framework selected. Also important is the development of a common understanding and shared knowledge of the language used in the supervision and evaluation of teachers. This enables a school leader to provide constructive feedback to a teacher and encourages effective coaching and mentoring.

Instructional leaders need to develop strategies for supporting teachers and improving on their teaching throughout their professional careers. Expectations must be raised, but resources and leadership are necessary components to improving teacher performance in the classroom. What is important is the process and implementation of how to evaluate and supervise teachers. The primary focus must be on how they grow in expertise and become more effective in their classrooms. These school leader action steps assist in setting the implementation:

- Goal setting is a collaborative process and the focus is on increased teacher effectiveness.
- There are high expectations set for effective teaching and student learning.

- Failure is not accepted and intervention is the norm. All students can learn.
- There is acknowledgment, alignment, and support of district goals by all stakeholders.
- There is sustained monitoring of achievement and instructional goals based on the analysis of relevant data.
- There is ongoing support and allocation of resources to support the goals for achievement and instruction.

All of these actions can be implemented collaboratively whether working with individual teachers, groups, or organizations. A superintendent and board of education should set high student achievement goals for the district and each student sub-group. These goals must be communicated effectively to school principals and teachers. Annual performance goals should be tied to student achievement goals identified for their school.

It is important that district and school leaders seek board of education support and approval of district goals. School leaders need to be held accountable for teacher and student performance. Using data and analyzing results will provide a platform for setting or adjusting instructional goals over time. Finally, school and district leaders need to work as a team to create and allocate funding and resources to support the whole learning and growth process.

Often districts lack a strong relationship between the evaluation and supervision processes. Basically, the traditional process has been time intensive without much impact on teacher effectiveness and, subsequently, increased student performance. Adult learning theory suggests adults learn best by active engagement. Teachers benefit best in a well-defined and relevant supervision and evaluation process when they are active and reflective participants.

INDIVIDUAL PROFESSIONAL LEARNING AND GROWTH PLANS

Using the Learning Forward *Standards for Professional Learning* (2011) can provide a more robust supervision and evaluation process for teachers. First, there is the need to create a learning organization with identified learning communities at grade and content levels committed to continual improvement, collective responsibility, and goal alignment.

Allotting time and resources for collaboration by these groups on a regular basis during the school year is a requirement and ongoing commitment. In addition, training in team skills will assist with the transformation of the culture and climate of the individual, group, and organization. It is also important to build an accountability process for professional learning communities whereby agendas, minutes, actions taken, and issues discussed are provided to school leaders and team members for review.

School and teacher leaders must act as instructional leaders. They must articulate the overall vision and mission of the district. The primary goal must be that all students have the opportunity to master the knowledge and skills identified in an articulated curriculum aligned with national and state standards. Finally, there is a strong belief that all teachers and students are lifelong learners. A core value of continual improvement is the underlying foundation of the school and district as a professional learning community.

Even though each teacher is looked upon as a lifelong learner in a professional learning community, it is important to differentiate the need for intensity for supervision and evaluation of teachers. Teachers whose level of performance is rated as "meets" or "proficient" could be evaluated every other year and encouraged to continue to grow and learn throughout their careers. However, they could be used to mentor and coach those teachers who need improvement or who are placed in remediation plans. Teachers who meet or are proficient could be evaluated every other year and encouraged to continue to grow so that they can reach a distinguished performance level.

New teachers who need much coaching and mentoring and those teachers rated as unsatisfactory or needs improvement should be monitored more closely on an annual basis. If their status remains unchanged, consideration should be given to dismissal because they do not have the ability to grow or improve or they are choosing not to grow professionally.

When teachers are ineffective in the classroom, they affect student achievement in a negative way. Equity is the issue. It is unfair to the students assigned to an ineffective teacher because they will not have the same achievement levels as other peers who have been assigned to a more effective teacher. Their rate of growth will slow or remain stagnant in that subject or grade level.

District and school leaders need to have the moral courage to deal with these teachers. It is an unpleasant task but one that needs to be carried out if the vision of a learning organization is lifelong learners. Instructional leaders must ensure that all children are receiving an equal opportunity to learn with an effective teacher in their classroom.

A clinical supervision model using the learning and growth plan processes would look somewhat different than the traditional clinical supervision model. The clinical model of teacher evaluation is outlined in detail in chapter 6. A modified clinical model with the intent of ongoing teacher growth and learning has several steps.

Informal Classroom Walk-Throughs

A written notification to the teacher about an evaluation would be given during the first month of the school year. School leaders who are involved in supervising and evaluating teachers would use a process that would provide opportunities for them to be in the classrooms more often for shorter periods of time throughout the year. It makes sense that an instructional leader would make short unannounced visits followed with immediate feedback to all teachers.

A continual dialogue about teaching and learning would be ongoing between evaluator and teacher. The dialogue between teachers and evaluators would be instrumental in helping to build professional relationships and encourage the exchange of ideas about teaching and learning. Multiple informal walk-throughs would be conducted on a regular basis throughout the process and continue throughout the school year. It is suggested to begin with less as a way to get started and work up to at least ten observations as a goal.

Four walk-throughs of at least ten to fifteen minutes would be required before the pre-conference so that the evaluator would be able to get an idea of the culture and climate of the teacher's classroom. It is not suggested that one use a checklist for this type of walk-through. Checklists can be a distraction and may keep the evaluator from focusing on the activity in the classroom while he or she is in there.

The short observations and few notes taken during the process should provide the evaluator with some talking points about possible areas of focus during the pre-conference with the teacher. For example, perhaps in the evaluator's walk-through, he or she noticed that the teacher questions appeared to be an area for discussion because most of the questions appeared to be at lower cognitive levels. That may become the focus of the evaluator's conversation with the teacher.

Sharing the data the evaluator has collected during his or her informal observations in the classroom and working together to identify this as an area in need of improvement would help facilitate the transition to the formal evaluation process. Identifying the area of focus together encourages teacher self-assessment and reflection.

The evaluator would discuss this area as a focus for the formal observation of the teacher and other walk-throughs during the year. The evaluator could also share with the teacher the process tool that he or she would use to collect hard data as evidence of the levels of teacher questions during the lesson. It is also important to discuss the difference between a running narrative and this focused type of observation and how the data will be collected using process tools.

Pre-Observation Conference

The pre-conference has a slightly different approach using the professional learning and growth model. The teacher will bring ideas for the development of a lesson plan with objectives and possible activities that the evaluator might observe. The data collected during the four walk-throughs will also be discussed. A focus area will be targeted as an area for observation based on the walk-through data. The evaluator will collaborate with the teacher to design a process tool to collect data on the mutually agreed upon area of focus. These areas of focus would begin the dialogue for a professional learning plan.

After the pre-conference, the teacher will submit a detailed lesson plan with goals and objectives that are aligned with standards. This becomes the lesson that will be observed during the formal observation. Both evaluator and teacher agree upon the lesson plan to be observed.

Measuring Teacher Outputs with Process Tools

Before evaluators begin the formal observation, they will need to decide on how to measure outputs (teacher performance and student performance). The most effective method to gather evidence in the form of hard data is to use process tools that will yield the number of times a certain behavior you are looking for occurred during the formal observation.

Figure 4.3, provides an example of a checklist of *cognitive levels of questioning* for teacher observation. When a teacher asks a question, the

| Observer: _____ | Teacher: _____ |
| Date & Time: _____ | Class: _____ |

	Q1	Q2	Q3	Q4	Q5	Q6	Q7	Q8	Q9	Q10
Levels										
Remembering										
Understanding										
Applying										
Analyzing										
Evaluating										
Creating										

Comments:

Figure 4.3. Checklist of Cognitive Levels of Questioning for Teacher Observation

evaluator would determine the level of the question asked. This yields unbiased evidence that can be used in the post-conference discussion of the teacher's performance.

Formal Observation

The observation should be at least forty-five to sixty minutes long. Data are gathered using the process tools, notes, forms, or any other type of data-gathering tool. This allows the evaluator to focus on the area identified in the pre-observation conference.

Data Collection and Analysis

After the data have been collected, the observer should conduct an analysis of the data and what it means. It is helpful to use percentages or other statistical vocabulary to provide relevant data to the teacher as evidence. Using this kind of evidence ensures that the teacher evaluation performance level is not based on opinion or bias.

If eight of the ten teacher questions were recorded as being at a low cognitive level, the evidence indicates that this is an area for improvement. It is hard to argue with evidence collected in this manner. It is also useful for the teacher and evaluator as they prepare a professional learning and growth plan that will increase teacher effectiveness in this area.

Post-Observation Conference with Professional Learning and Growth Plan

At the post-observation conference, the evaluator and the teacher will meet to examine and discuss the clinical notes and data taken by the observer. From this discussion they will craft an individual professional learning and growth plan. The evaluator's recommendations to the teacher are based upon research-based best practices that improve teacher effectiveness. An individual learning and growth plan includes the following elements: *goals, action steps, a time line, the person(s) responsible, evaluation,* and *documentation for evidence of completion* of each goal and action step.

The individualized learning plan can be used to guide the teacher through renewal, training, or content development. The power of developing an individualized plan is that each teacher is evaluated and his or her performance is rated. For example, using the Danielson framework, a teacher could be rated as needs improvement in *domain 3: classroom instruction, questioning techniques.* An individualized plan could be developed for this teacher with goals and action steps designed to improve the teacher's questioning techniques.

Even if a teacher were distinguished or proficient, an individualized learning plan could be developed collaboratively by the evaluator to target an area of growth. Every teacher, no matter what the performance level, would continue to grow and learn during his or her career. This is the essence of a continual improvement process.

As in any learning organization, all teachers will be required to continue to learn and improve and become more effective. This will have an effect on the entire district and school as each teacher becomes more effective. The whole professional growth and learning community (individuals, schools, and district) will shift on the continuum to the right demonstrating improvement not only individually but also collectively.

Accountability and more administrative "hands-on" coaching and mentoring are needed to successfully improve instruction and increase teacher effectiveness. School leaders should be observing teachers in classrooms at least 50 percent of the time—preferably 75 percent. Immediate follow-up constructive feedback also should be given. Tapping the talent and expertise of distinguished teachers to coach and mentor those teachers who are unsatisfactory, need improvement, or proficient is a powerful way to create a *professional learning and growth community.*

DIFFERENTIATING PROFESSIONAL GROWTH AND LEARNING PLANS

There are many different types of sub-groups in a district and school. A few of the more common ones include:

- Novice teachers
- Content area teachers
- Specialists: instructional coaches, reading specialists, interventionists, and special education, among others.
- Nurses, counselors, deans, social workers
- District and school administrators

The same *Standards for Professional Learning* need to be applied to these sub-groups within a district or a school. Leaders who are planning professional learning should develop, advocate, and create support systems for professional learning. They should prioritize, monitor, and coordinate resources and make them available for each group. Multiple forms and sources of data should be used to identify needs, plan accordingly, assess, and evaluate the professional learning taking place in each group.

Theories, research, and models of human learning should be used to achieve the intended outcomes. The application of research to change and professional learning should be applied with sustained support during implementation until long-term change is embedded in the culture. The outcomes should align with educator performance and student curriculum standards. Chapter 7 outlines and provides an example of an effective middle school action plan for professional learning and growth.

PROFESSIONAL LEARNING AND GROWTH PLANS FOR DISTRICTS

District administrators need to make sure that they comply with federal and state mandates because training at the district level is somewhat guided by these mandates. For example, some district administrators might require all faculty and staff members to participate in CPR training as a safety precaution in case they encounter a situation where they need to administer this to an individual in distress on school property. Another example might be the requirement for new faculty and staff members to attend a weeklong induction program to learn about health benefits, payroll information, and district policies.

In addition, each school may also require a two-day induction program to talk about requirements and policies in its building. During this time, administration, faculty, and staff may share information and training regarding a variety of issues including new curriculum guidelines and standards.

SUMMARY

As opposed to the traditional clinical model of supervision and evaluation, an improved evaluation process that focuses on a cycle of observations along with a professional learning plan is suggested. The *professional learning and growth evaluation model* requires evaluators to be observing teachers in classrooms 50 to 75 percent of their time. They should act in the role of coaches and mentors and give responsive constructive feedback. This allows evaluators who are wearing their "supervision hat" to give teachers immediate feedback.

Conducting walk-throughs will create a healthier relationship between the evaluator and teacher when it is time for a formal evaluation. The evaluator already has a good idea of the teachers' areas of strength and areas for growth, having seen them teach many times. So instead of one or two formal evaluations during the evaluation cycle that yields limited information about the teacher's effectiveness, the evaluator can work collaboratively with the teacher to develop an individualized *professional learning and growth plan* at the end of the post-conference.

The individualized professional learning and growth plans lead to the development of a *professional learning and growth community*. The vision for a school must be to develop a culture that believes in lifelong learning for faculty, staff, and students. It is important for school and district leaders to work with teachers to implement organizational structures and resources for the development of a *professional learning and growth community*.

A *professional learning and growth community* promotes lifelong learning and continual improvement. This results in an increase in effective teaching and student achievement. Every child deserves to be in a classroom with a highly effective teacher.

CASE STUDY

Ms. Jones was very excited about her appointment as the new principal in a large K–8 building (750 students and 60 certified teachers) in a small rural district. She came in early in the summer to read through the sixty certified teachers' personnel files. What she found was a surprise! All sixty of her teachers had been rated as "outstanding" over the past fifteen years. The faculty had never been engaged in the planning of curriculum and instruction. In fact, there were no organizational structures in place for any kind of collaborative work. They referred to the old principal as "the cruise director" because he liked to plan parties, serve food, and tell jokes!

As the new principal, Ms. Jones was faced with making some decisions about teacher evaluation. As the new instructional leader, where would you begin? How would you develop a comprehensive evaluation plan for teachers? How would you go about bringing about a change in the school climate and culture? When, where, and how would you begin? Develop a one-year action plan to begin the change process for a professional learning community.

EXERCISES AND DISCUSSION QUESTIONS

1. Building a learning community in a school is the key to a collaborative culture. As an instructional leader, where would you begin?

How would you encourage and facilitate a more *reflective practice* by your teachers?

2. Why is it important for a district to select a framework for teaching that can be used by all teachers, evaluators, and supervisors when discussing and evaluating teacher effectiveness? How does this framework help teachers, supervisors, and evaluators to become more effective?

3. How is the professional learning and growth evaluation process different from the traditional model of professional development? What is unique about the process? How will this collaborative system affect student performance?

4. What is the first step to take when differentiating professional development? What groups would you identify in your school? How would you identify their needs? What data would you analyze?

REFERENCES

Danielson, C. (2007). *Enhancing professional practice: A framework for teaching.* (2nd ed.). Alexandria, VA: Association for Supervision and Curriculum Development.

Dean, C., Hubbel, E., Pitler, H., & Stone, B. (2012). *Classroom instruction that works* (2nd ed.). Alexandria, VA: Association for Supervision and Curriculum Development.

DuFour, R., and Marzano, R. (2011). *Leaders of learning: How district, school and classroom leaders improve student achievement.* Bloomington, IN: Solution Tree Press.

Marshall, K. (2013). *Rethinking teacher supervision and evaluation: How to work smart, build collaboration, and close the achievement gap* (2nd ed.). San Francisco, CA: Jossey-Bass.

Senge, P. (1990). *The fifth discipline: The art and practice of the learning organization.* New York: Currency Doubleday.

Standards for Professional Learning. (2011). Canton, Ohio: Learning Forward

5

Building a Framework for Professional Learning and Growth

OBJECTIVES

At the conclusion of this chapter you will be able to:

1. Understand how to develop and implement a professional learning and growth model (ELCC 1, 2, 3, 5, 6; ISLCC 1, 2, 3, 5, 6; InTASC 2, 3, 7; Learning Forward Standards).
2. Apply the Learning Forward Standards, and be able to develop professional learning and growth plans (ELCC 1, 2, 3, 5, 6; ISLCC 1, 2, 3, 5, 6; InTASC 2, 3, 7; Learning Forward Standards).
3. Review an effective leadership model for professional learning and growth, and understand how it is used to empower and reinforce teacher improvement (ELCC 1, 2, 3, 5, 6; ISLCC 1, 2, 3, 5, 6; InTASC 2, 3, 7; Learning Forward Standards).

PROFESSIONAL LEARNING AND GROWTH IMPLEMENTATION MODEL

Thus far, this book has focused on understanding models and standards for effective teaching. The role and differentiation of professional learning and growth were defined and outlined, but how do you implement a professional learning and growth model? How can we be sure teachers will accept it? Who should be involved? And, how can we ensure the model will be successful?

Let's start by examining a *professional learning and growth* (PLG) *implementation model* (see Figure 5.1). This PLG model is designed to help district and school leaders implement a plan through a systematic approach, which includes all stakeholders (teachers, school and district leaders, team leaders, board members, parents, and community members) through a collaborative, decision-making process. The PLG implementation model consists of a five-phase process of planning, assessing, preparing, implementing, and evaluating.

The PLG model entails a comprehensive, step-by-step process. It requires the development of a professional learning and growth climate. It includes alignment of all members of the school community in bringing about meaningful school change. This process can be led by the district leader or in conjunction with an outside consultant. The consultant can be useful in assisting school leaders with the implementation effort and can bring an independent, unbiased perspective to the team.

The first phase, *planning*, begins with the district leader forming a *steering committee* to guide the process. This team might consist of the district assistant superintendent for curriculum and instruction (who might also chair the committee), building principals, assistant principals, teacher leaders, teachers, and other staff members. It also might be possible, depending upon the unique aspects of the school district, to include board members, parents, union representatives, and community members.

The purpose of this steering committee is to understand the entire professional learning and growth process, provide inspiration and direction for the change process, overcome roadblocks and resistance, deal with union issues, maintain communications among all stakeholders, and provide resource support (e.g., finances, materials, facilities, and time). The committee also can be very useful as a communication network in keeping everyone informed throughout the process.

The first action might be to conduct a team-building session for the committee members. This session can help to build morale and relationships, establish common values and goals, clarify roles and expectations, determine communication processes, and develop ground rules in working together. The team-building session can help to provide an understanding of the different personalities of the team members and help identify the team's strengths and weaknesses.

The committee could also work collaboratively to develop alignment with the school improvement plans and the district goals. The committee could focus on the development of building the capacity of members within the school's professional learning community. The desired outcome could be a goal to transform the district and school culture from a

Professional Learning and Growth (PLG) Implementation Model

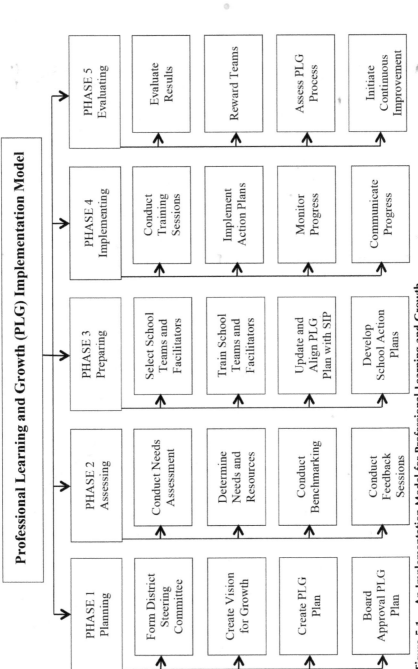

PHASE 1 Planning	PHASE 2 Assessing	PHASE 3 Preparing	PHASE 4 Implementing	PHASE 5 Evaluating
Form District Steering Committee	Conduct Needs Assessment	Select School Teams and Facilitators	Conduct Training Sessions	Evaluate Results
Create Vision for Growth	Determine Needs and Resources	Train School Teams and Facilitators	Implement Action Plans	Reward Teams
Create PLG Plan	Conduct Benchmarking	Update and Align PLG Plan with SIP	Monitor Progress	Assess PLG Process
Board Approval PLG Plan	Conduct Feedback Sessions	Develop School Action Plans	Communicate Progress	Initiate Continuous Improvement

Figure 5.1.   An Implementation Model for Professional Learning and Growth

traditional culture where teachers typically work mostly in isolation to a professional learning and growth community with shared aspirations, goals, and outcomes.

The first step in this *planning phase* is to develop a clear *vision* for professional growth and learning that reflects the needs of the students, faculty, and community. This vision needs to represent a crystallized, long-range picture of what the professional learning and growth model should accomplish. The development of this vision may require the use of one or more vision-building sessions to create the vision. It can also serve to further build interpersonal relationships and trust among the team members. Essentially, the vision becomes the foundation of common expectations for the PLG implementation process.

For example, Figure 5.2 illustrates a *professional learning and growth (PLG) framework* for achieving a vision of increasing *student performance*. This framework consists of three components: the teacher evaluation model, supervision, and evaluation. The teacher evaluation component might include one of the research-based models or a custom-developed model by the district (refer to chapter 2).

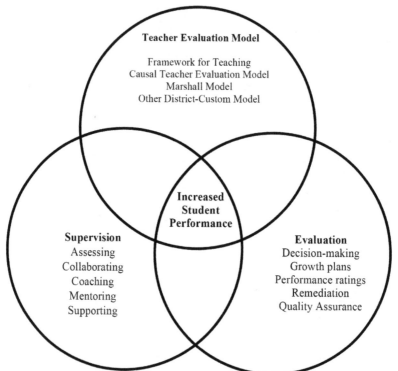

Figure 5.2 Professional Learning and Growth Framework for Increased Student Performance

The supervision and evaluation components of the PLG framework would include assessing, collaborating, coaching, mentoring, remediating, accountability, performance ratings, and quality assurance. These components were described in previous chapters. The PLG framework also can be useful as a visual method for all stakeholders to understand the components of a professional learning and growth framework.

After the *vision* has been established, the steering committee should integrate the vision into an *operational PLG plan*, which includes organizational goals aligned with state, district, and school goals. The plan also must be aligned with the evaluation model chosen by the district, whether it is a custom model or one from other research-based models in the field. This operational plan also should include a comprehensive strategy for achieving student improvement and how to implement the professional learning and growth model chosen.

An effective operational plan should include the vision, major goals, key strategies, resources, and a realistic timetable. It should identify those people who are responsible for the different steps of the process. The professional learning and growth model should be clear and understandable to everyone. Likewise, the roles and levels of authority of those involved in the implementation process should be clear. The operational PLG plan must be reviewed with and approved by the district board of education before moving forward to actual implementation.

The school PLG plan can be independent of the *school improvement plan* (SIP), a revision of it, or an addendum to it depending upon the needs of the school and the district. For example, if the school is in the beginning phases of developing the SIP, then it probably makes sense to include a PLG plan in the SIP. However, if the SIP has already been developed, it may be sensible to revise the SIP based upon the PLG plan and process.

Once the operational plan is completed and approved by the board of education, the steering committee should move into phase two, assessing the district and schools. The purpose of this phase, *assessing*, is to clearly identify the district and the school's strengths and areas in need of improvement (i.e., the major educational problems, gaps, and needs of the district and schools). A needs assessment can be designed to measure people's opinions and perceptions regarding the current evaluation system, professional development programs, human resources, supporting systems, technology, facilities, student performance outcomes, state and federal expectations, and teacher competencies.

This information can be collected through online needs assessment surveys, staff interviews, school data analysis, and analysis of student performance scores. For example, in assessing student performance, one could examine a grade four school PLC studying math concepts and skills. The PLC review of past student performance discovers math skills in adding, subtracting, and multiplying fractions is below state standards and the district-expected student performance levels. This becomes a targeted area for the school and district needs assessment and could become a goal for future professional learning plans.

Another example could be a high school PLC in science. The PLC analysis of student performance data shows that grade ten students are not meeting expected performance in understanding key biology vocabulary. Action steps could be developed for increasing student scientific vocabulary knowledge. These action steps could be turned into possible goals for future individual professional learning and growth plans. Such steps could guide principals, department chairs, team leaders, and teachers in leading a review or redesign of the district biology program.

Once the steering committee collects, analyzes, and reviews the data from the needs assessment, the next step is to determine the needs and resources for the district and schools. Based on the SIP and the district strategic plan, strengths and areas in need of improvement can be targeted for action plan development.

At this point in the process, the steering committee will need to begin to conduct *benchmarking*. This is a process of identifying those best practices resulting in increased student performance used by other schools and districts during the implementation of professional learning growth plans. These benchmarked indicators can help to guide the school teams as they develop action plans.

An overall assessment report (i.e., identifying needs of the school) should then be prepared for the entire district and each school. The committee should ensure anonymity and openness among the respondents. Keeping people informed during this stage of the process can help ensure buy-in and future success.

Once the assessment report is prepared, a series of *feedback sessions* might be held to engage all stakeholders and discuss the results. The feedback sessions allow everyone to understand the outcomes of the needs assessments, clarify issues, and allow participants to ask questions about the PLG implementation process. It is important to provide opportunities for stakeholders to identify problem areas in the plan. Overcoming resistance is important to a successful implementation process. Stakeholders do not want to feel that they are left out of the decision-making process. Once the feedback sessions have been held, the next step is phase three, *preparing*.

The purpose of phase three is to provide the necessary resources and training needed to implement the professional learning model and plan. *School action teams* should be selected from various stakeholders at the district, school, and department or grade levels. Teams should also consist of personnel from technology, human resource, teaching, and administration, among others. The more broadly based the action teams, the more likelihood of buy-in from the stakeholders.

The concept and intention of these action teams are similar to *professional learning communities* (PLC) where members collaboratively work together in planning and implementing the PLG plan. Collaboration helps to provide a synergistic approach to brainstorming, problem solving, and decision making during this phase.

Also, during this phase, the team members need to thoroughly understand the components of the professional learning and growth evaluation model. These key components include the professional domains (i.e., classroom strategies, assessment, family and community outreach); elements of the model; levels and ratings of performance, goals, and objectives; expected professional learning outcomes; evaluation and supervision processes; technology use; and other support systems.

For example, in the benchmarking process, the professional learning model may be identified as best practice, but if the human resource and technology staff members are not directly involved, the entire model could fail simply because it can't be supported by the current technology and human resource support systems. These systems may need to be upgraded, improved, or replaced. They need to be dynamic, provide real-time data, and include a shared databased system that integrates employee information, position, financial compensation, certification, endorsements, credentials, past evaluations, or other unique features relevant to the needs of the district.

Each *action team* should consist of various stakeholders who have expertise in a given area and who genuinely desire to work to implement the PLG plan. In addition to establishing action teams, a pool of *facilitators* might be needed. These facilitators are typically stakeholders who are trained in group-processing techniques. Facilitators can act as group leaders in conducting the sessions and could be members of the steering committee. They also can be valuable in keeping the action teams on task, developing the meeting agendas and minutes, and acting as a communication link with the steering committee and stakeholders of the school.

Once the teams and facilitators have been established, each team should develop a work plan and determine how the plan should operate. And, if necessary, the school improvement plan (SIP) could be updated. The last step in the preparing phase is *developing the action plan*. In other words, how is the PLG model going to be "rolled out?" For example, the various teams at the school level should have a detailed action plan for implementation, needed resources, people involved, budget, and a timetable. The steering committee might give each team a common format or template to use in preparing the action plan.

Phase four, *implementing*, consists of executing the actual professional learning model within the entire school district. Once the PLG plan is implemented, it should be monitored and progress communicated to all stakeholders. The key step in phase four is conducting training sessions so that staff members understand the processes, the steps in the rollout, the expected outcomes, and the communication links. Communication is critical to this process, and it is easy for this step to be overlooked. Common communication methods may include staff meetings, newsletters, department meetings, e-mails, blogs, web news sites, parent letters, and/or special update sessions.

The last phase, *evaluating*, consists of the school action teams working with the steering committee in evaluating the results of the rollout and implementation. Follow-up surveys, individual and group interviews, student academic assessments, test scores, and benchmarking comparisons can be used as part of this process. This stage can be considered *data-driven decision making* to identify issues that need immediate correction and determine what actions require revision to meet student learning and organizational needs.

The final steps involve *initiating continual improvements* to the PLG framework and assessing results. In this step, it is important to reward teams and celebrate successes. Also, the team should reassess the entire process and make necessary improvements. Results of actions should be documented and shared with all stakeholders. Based upon review and evaluation of the PLG implementation process and the outcomes, the steering committee may revise or alter steps and/or actions within the framework processes.

DEVELOPING INDIVIDUAL PROFESSIONAL LEARNING PLANS

Broadly defined, the primary work of a professional learning and growth community is to help teachers become more effective. The outcome would be students achieving at a higher performance level. PLG plans provide opportunities for all members of the learning community to engage in a *professional dialogue*. The dialogue must focus on the development of an enriching curriculum and effective implementation of district-selected, research-based instructional strategies.

For a PLG model to be successful, all district and school leaders, teachers, and staff should develop professional learning plans. It must start with the superintendent who needs to model and develop a *superintendent professional learning and growth plan* (see appendix E). This plan could be guided by the ISLCC standards (see appendix B). For example, the superintendent plan might include the goals, action steps, time lines, resources, person(s) responsible, and evidence of completion for each of the standards.

When the plan is completed, the superintendent should meet with the president of the board of education to review the plan. The president of the board of education and the superintendent would then present the plan to the entire board, usually at a spring board meeting during closed session. The board would then vote to accept the plan and the implementation process would begin. There is usually a midyear update to the board by the superintendent.

Typically, at the end of the school year, the board of education evaluates the superintendent. The board president would work with the superintendent to gather evidence for each goal and the action steps taken in the professional learning and growth plan to demonstrate successful completion. The superintendent's goals should be directly linked to the three, mutually agreed upon key indicators for district and school success that were shared with the board of education, faculty, staff, parents, and community.

Generally, superintendents are evaluated by the board of education annually. Most superintendents have multiyear contracts. Contracts are usually two, three, or five years in length. A level of performance is determined during the board evaluation process. In a proactive leadership model for professional learning and growth, the board of education should determine the superintendent's performance by rating each area using a scale such as *distinguished, satisfactory, needs improvement,* or *unsatisfactory* for each of the indicators used to measure student growth. For example, it may be best to set student performance outcomes and goals for the duration of a three-year contract and then present annual evidence of progress made to meet those anticipated outcomes and goals.

District leaders should be required to build portfolios for each ISLCC standard and collect artifacts as evidence of completion of their goals and action steps. Examples of some artifacts that may be presented include multiple measures of student performance data, schedules of professional learning and growth team meetings, and samples of individual school leaders' learning and growth plans. Professional learning and growth plan activities demonstrating student growth also could be assessed and shared as artifacts. These could include testing data analysis by content areas or grade levels, instructional program evaluations, or culture and climate surveys.

It is also important that the superintendent, the board of education, school leaders, and various school community stakeholders participate in the strategic planning process. The strategic plan should be a minimum five-year cycle and reviewed yearly. Reviewing previous strategic plans, evaluating outcomes, and making key revisions assist in keeping the vision and mission of the district relevant and up to date.

By revisiting the district's values, vision, and mission, stakeholders can keep abreast of current research and trends that are important to student learning. Coming to consensus about core values and beliefs, and clearly articulating vision and mission will support the development of a common understanding and road map for all members of the communities served by the district. This will require the superintendent and district leaders to provide guidance and training for school leaders, faculty, and staff. Developing a common shared language about effective teaching and learning is essential. All leaders need a professional learning and growth plan to help them become more effective instructional leaders.

For example, a chief school business official (CSBO) can benefit from a professional learning and growth plan that focuses on providing sustained and equitable funding resources for the organization. The CSBO would work collaboratively to allocate funds to the areas of need identified by a principal and a school leadership team. A school need might include release time for professional growth in the area of math instruction. Principals may need to hire substitute teachers to allow teachers who are highly effective in teaching mathematics to observe, mentor, and coach less effective teachers.

Each school could be given a budget line item designating the funds for professional learning and growth. The CSBO could then be evaluated by the performance indicators used to measure student growth. The plan should also include goals with measurable outcomes related to school funding and budgeting.

Let's examine how we might construct a professional learning plan for principals. Their plan might include two goals based on the ISLLC standards 1 and 2 similar to those of the district leaders (see appendix E). An expected goal could be established for principals that would include nurturing and sustaining a culture of collaboration, trust, learning, and high academic expectations. The objective for the principal could be to work with teacher leaders, faculty, and staff in the school in creating a personalized and motivating learning environment for all students and staff.

Each principal could be expected to create a school climate that would provide an environment for learning and growth for all teachers and students. Principals would lead by developing and supporting the instructional and leadership capacity of the faculty and staff. There could be high expectations for achievement for all students regardless of their situation. Both informal and formal assessments could be used to determine whether students are making progress. Differentiation of instruction and other instruction interventions could be used to meet the individual needs of students who are not progressing. These interventions could become goals for professional learning plans.

For example, the superintendent could evaluate each principal every year by reviewing mutually agreed upon goals and action steps determined at the beginning of the school year. Student achievement data could be examined annually and analyzed to determine whether student performance in the school is improving. The survey data from faculty, staff, students, parents, and community members also could be used as an indicator to measure the principal's leadership skills, school/community relationships, and leadership performance.

How would a teacher professional learning and growth plan be developed? Similar to the professional learning and growth plans for district and school leaders, a teacher plan would be focused on increasing student performance. Appendix E includes a sample professional learning plan for a teacher. For example, a principal, teacher leader, department chair, or other evaluator could work with a classroom teacher to develop a professional learning and growth plan focused on student performance outcomes. One possible goal might come from the work of the PLC in which the teacher is a member.

The PLC has identified a problem with student performance in adding, subtracting, and multiplying fractions. The teacher and evaluator could develop and write a sub-goal in the area of instructional strategies that focus on re-teaching and reinforcing the understanding of fraction concepts. Perhaps the teacher could even work with another mentor teacher who has been successful in teaching fractions. A sub-goal could be written to include classroom visits where the teacher observes the mentor teacher as fractions are being taught.

Another sub-goal could include writing common classroom assessments in adding, subtracting, and multiplying fractions. The PLC could work to support each member while constructing authentic and relevant classroom assessments. The PLC would then work together to monitor and assess each student. All of these goals could become part of the teacher's individualized learning and growth plan.

After all, the primary goal for every teacher should be to professionally learn, grow, develop, and expand effective instructional methodology. Teachers can become more effective and students can achieve higher levels of performance through the use of a well-constructed PLG model. These types of plans become central to effective supervision and evaluation of teachers. Teachers would be working together to achieve what they cannot accomplish alone. The district and schools would evolve into professional learning and growth communities that support continual improvement and lifelong learning.

ACHIEVING SUCCESS THROUGH SHARED LEADERSHIP

Fundamental to the entire PLG process is the need for effective leadership. Successful school districts need to have collaborative and supportive superintendents and school leaders who are positive and effective communicators. They must be skilled coaches and mentors. They need to develop high expectations and permit faculty and staff flexibility in achieving mutually agreed upon student performance goals and outcomes approved by the board of education.

For example, the model outlined in Figure 5.3 can be useful for district and school leaders in providing the leadership needed for a PLG organization. This model integrates the key components of goals, performance, and best practices.

A school leader can be any individual in a school who evaluates or supervises teachers. This can include principals, assistant principals, teacher leaders, department heads, directors, deans, and grade level and

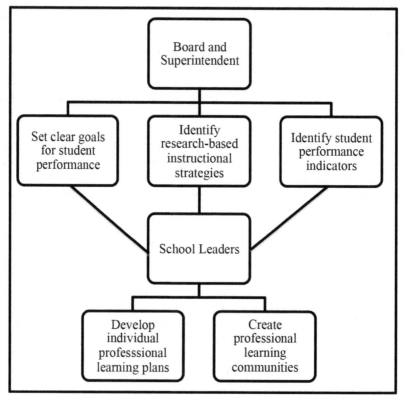

Figure 5.3. Leadership Model for Professional Learning and Growth

content area leaders. For example, the principal might develop a school leadership team composed of school leaders from the various departments and sub-groups in the school. The principal also could be the facilitator and a member of this team.

The teacher leaders selected by the principal to serve on this team could have some or all of the characteristics outlined in the ISLLC Leadership Standards (see appendix B) and the Teacher Leader Domains (see appendix D). Each teacher leader chosen by the principal should possess the following characteristics:

- Understand the principles of adult learning
- Know how to build a collaborative culture
- Promote professional learning and growth
- Develop professional learning and growth community plans
- Understand how to analyze and use data for school improvement
- Facilitate improvements in instruction and student learning
- Practice self-reflection and assessment
- Possess a deep knowledge and understanding about teaching and learning
- Desire to coach and mentor other colleagues

By virtue of their role among their colleagues, teacher leaders are facilitators for developing and improving instructional practices. They usually are the best of the teaching ranks and are highly trained and effective teachers.

Because teacher leaders become central to supporting and advancing professional learning and growth for peers, they also need a professional learning and growth plan. Appendix E contains a sample professional learning and growth plan for a teacher leader. Teacher leaders would be an added level of support in a shared leadership culture focused on professional learning and growth. The PLG culture encourages teachers to learn and grow together both individually and collectively. Research indicates that district and school leaders play a key role in creating conditions that will establish and sustain a professional learning and growth community (McLaughlin & Talbert, 2006).

Building the leadership capacity of a faculty can be done through visitations at schools where highly functioning professional learning and growth communities can be observed. Next, leaders should model and guide weekly meetings of groups as the group learns to function as a PLC. Gradually, the setting of agendas, analysis of relevant data, and development and monitoring of action plans and results shift from the leader to other participants.

This develops teacher capacity for shared leadership. Principals can share examples and celebrate teachers who have demonstrated leadership characteristics so that teachers can learn from each other. District and school leaders can encourage self-reflection on a continual basis.

In addition, the district and school leaders should meet on a regular basis to monitor the progress made in each school toward the goal of developing a professional learning and growth community. These leaders must clearly monitor and celebrate success in the three mutually agreed upon key indicators of success for the district and schools. PLG communities thrive when focused on:

1. attainable goals for student performance,
2. best practices research-based instructional strategies, and
3. realistic criteria that will be used to measure student performance.

SUMMARY

The outcome of increasing teacher effectiveness is improved student performance. Research indicates that strong district leadership has a significant impact on teacher effectiveness. Superintendents, boards of education, and school leaders should demand that every child have a highly effective teacher in the classroom.

The development of a high-functioning professional learning and growth community is founded on a collaborative and supportive leadership model. As illustrated in this model, district and school leaders should be positive in articulating the student performance goals set for the district, school, and student sub-groups. They also should publicly announce the performance indicators that will be used to measure student growth. They also should convey the research-based instructional strategies that classroom teachers need to use to teach the students. All of these elements are directed by mutually agreed upon criteria.

School leaders play a key role in the development of a professional learning and growth community. They will wear two hats: the supervision hat and the evaluation hat. During the evaluation year the evaluator will conduct a formal evaluation of the teacher and determine a performance rating. During the formal evaluation, the evaluator will work collaboratively with the teacher to develop an individual professional learning and growth plan, and then supervise the teacher's performance.

Plans will differ depending on the performance rating of the teachers and whether they have tenure or not. Teachers who receive a rating of needs improvement or unsatisfactory should receive plans developed as required by state or contract legal requirements. During supervision, a supervisor should support teachers by acting as a coach and mentor. The supervisor should provide resources and encouragement as teachers complete their professional learning and growth plan. Teacher leaders can be called upon to coach and mentor fellow colleagues.

All members of each school's PLG community can become members of the district's collective PLG community. No longer should teachers work in isolation. Educators throughout the district will be working together as a professional learning and growth community to achieve what they cannot accomplish alone.

CASE STUDY

You are the new principal at Bunn Middle School. Your band teacher has been on the faculty for twenty years. The band has been experiencing yearly decreases in enrollment for the past five years. He is having documented discipline and student attendance issues. His attitude is very negative in the teachers' lunchroom, and he complains about his students, parents, and other faculty members, as well as the principal. When asked to do anything other than teach band, he declines. Each morning, just as the final bell is ringing for first period, he drives into the parking lot and runs to his classroom. After school, he stands in the cafeteria staring at the clock until the dismissal bell rings.

This is his tenured teacher evaluation year. You have observed him during three classroom visits, made frequent walk-throughs, and made several drop-in visits. In his summative evaluation you rated him as "needs improvement." You have identified instructional strategies, collegial relationships, and classroom management as three areas in need of improvement. Develop an individual professional learning and growth plan for this teacher. What outcomes do you expect for teacher behaviors and student behaviors? What ongoing professional growth activities do you anticipate he may need?

EXERCISES AND DISCUSSION QUESTIONS

1. Describe the climate and culture of a professional learning and growth community. How may it be different from the climate and culture of a traditional school without a professional and growth community?
2. Describe effective leadership in a PLG model. How may this leadership affect teacher effectiveness?

3. Analyze your school and how the leaders function. Outline a leadership theory that describes how your school leaders function and what effect it has on teacher effectiveness.
4. Define the basic steps in implementing a professional learning and growth plan.
5. How would you begin to implement a professional learning and growth model for your own district?

REFERENCES

McLaughlin, M., and Talbert, J. (2006). *Building school-based teacher learning communities: Professional strategies to improve student achievement.* New York: Teachers College Press.

6

✝

Teacher Evaluation and Professional Growth

OBJECTIVES

At the conclusion of this chapter you will be able to:

1. Understand state mandates and management and union relationships as related to teacher evaluations (ELCC 1, 3; ISLLC 1, 3; TLEC 1, 3; InTASC 2, 3, 7; Learning Forward Standards).
2. Understand strategies of goal setting as used with the teacher evaluation process and professional growth (ELCC 1, 3; ISLLC 1, 3; TLEC 1, 3; InTASC 2, 7; Learning Forward Standards).
3. Describe state and federal laws affecting teacher coaching and evaluations (ELCC 1, 1, 3; ISLLC 1, 3, TLEC 1, 3; InTASC 2, 3, 7; Learning Forward Standards).
4. Describe methods of conducting performance evaluations that are legally compliant (ELCC 1; ISLLC 1, 3; TLEC 1, 3; InTASC 3, 7; Learning Forward Standards).

STATE MANDATES AND TEACHER EVALUATIONS

Teacher evaluation in the United States continues to be an evolving process. Significant changes are being implemented that place greater emphasis on using multiple measures of assessment and professional learning and growth of teachers. Most of the states require objective measures of student performance such as classroom observations of teacher performance and actual student growth. Likewise, states are requiring that teachers receive professional development and coaching to help improve identified deficiencies.

The *National Council on Teacher Quality* (NCTQ) conducted an extensive study of teacher evaluations and effectiveness and identified several policies that states are requiring in the teacher evaluation program. Figure 6.1 illustrates several of the policies and percentage of states that connect these policies to evaluations of effectiveness. The trend is that states are including increased requirements for teacher accountability, professional learning and growth, student performance, and collaborative evaluations.

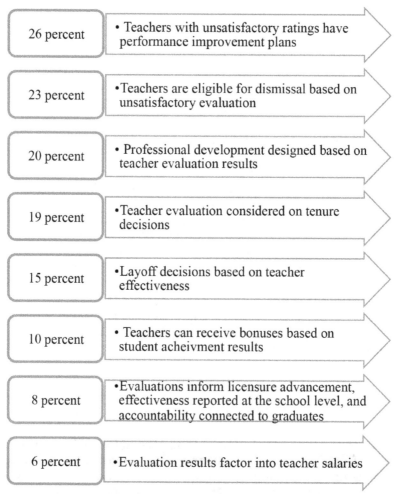

26 percent	• Teachers with unsatisfactory ratings have performance improvement plans
23 percent	•Teachers are eligible for dismissal based on unsatisfactory evaluation
20 percent	• Professional development designed based on teacher evaluation results
19 percent	•Teacher evaluation considered on tenure decisions
15 percent	•Layoff decisions based on teacher effectiveness
10 percent	• Teachers can receive bonuses based on student acheivment results
8 percent	•Evaluations inform licensure advancement, effectiveness reported at the school level, and accountability connected to graduates
6 percent	•Evaluation results factor into teacher salaries

Figure 6.1. Percent of States with Policies Connected to Evaluations

Source: Permission granted from National Council on Teacher Quality, 2013

Once the vision has been established the *major goals* are developed. These major goals are often written using SMART criteria—*specific, measurable, attainable, realistic,* and *timely.* The major goals are often directed to areas such as student performance, graduation rates, discipline, and attendance.

Once the major goals have been written, *key strategies* must be developed. A goal cannot be done. For example, if someone wants to become a millionaire, the *key strategy* outlines the process in how to get the money. If a major school goal is to improve student standardized performance, then actions need to be established to accomplish the goal.

Included within the key strategy should be well-written *key performance indicators* (KPIs), or *metrics.* These KPIs are the scorecards upon which the performance level is to be established. For example, if the major goal is to improve students' technological knowledge of software applications, then the key strategy might be to provide online training for the students with a key performance indicator of achieving 50 percent competency within three months.

The entire process then concludes with an evaluation of the teachers and others in how well they have accomplished the major goals. Teacher evaluation programs that include a goal-setting component might also be called *performance-based goals* or *student learning objectives* (SLOs). These performance-based goals are based on student progress and are generally aligned with curriculum and instruction standards.

Many school districts also connect the performance goals to a district teaching framework. For example, the goals could be written to support the domains of the teaching framework: planning and preparation, classroom environment, instruction, and professional responsibilities (Danielson, 2007). The State of Ohio has adopted a goal-setting process that incorporates a self-assessment and analysis of student data (Ohio Teacher Evaluation System, 2011).

CONDUCTING SUMMATIVE PERFORMANCE EVALUATIONS

In many school districts in the United States, performance evaluations are conducted by administrators or trained teacher evaluators. For example, in the State of Illinois, all teacher evaluators must complete and pass the teacher evaluator training program, as provided by the *Performance Evaluation Reform Act* (PERA) of 2010.

Part of the evaluation must include an assessment of teacher performance and student growth. Key factors of this legislation include teacher evaluator proficiency, rubrics, performance standards, observation, collaboration, reflection, evaluation, and alignment of teacher performance to student growth.

In addition, performance evaluations have increased in use because of the emphasis on performance accountability and standards. Using the performance evaluation process can be an important tool in helping to improve the performance of all teachers and staff within the school district.

There are many reasons for conducting performance evaluations (see Figure 6.2). The performance evaluation should not be a single-purpose process whereby the teacher leader quickly completes a form, holds a brief appraisal session, files the form, and then goes back to business as usual. The teacher leader should not consider the performance evaluation as busywork or as a *compliance exercise* just to satisfy school district or legal requirements.

This feeling by teacher evaluators may exist when evaluating tenured faculty. Some teacher leaders may feel handicapped in evaluating low-performing, tenured teachers when union contractual obstacles make it difficult to terminate a tenured teacher. Teacher evaluators should not take the easy way out and complete a quick or shallow performance review.

Performance evaluations can be a mechanism for accomplishing many goals. One reason for the evaluation is to give genuine constructive performance feedback to the employee, which can reinforce good performance and identify areas in need of improvement. The review session also can provide an opportunity to motivate employees through intrinsic verbal praise and act as a basis for extrinsic rewards such as salary increases and bonuses.

The performance evaluation session can serve to help promote communications, review respective performance, and develop continual

1. Provide performance feedback
2. Help motivate people
3. Promote communications
4. Use as a basis for staff development
5. Validate and document performance
6. Document performance problems
7. Comply with legal mandates
8. Provide rewards for people

Figure 6.2.   **Reasons for Conducting Performance Evaluations**

improvement plans for the future. This communication can serve as a basis for further developing people by establishing goals and gaining input that can help the entire organization.

Another reason for conducting the performance evaluation session is to validate and document performance of employees. This documentation serves as a record for employee performance, which is needed when there is a need to terminate the employee in the future. Complying with legal and district policies is another reason to document performance problems. Lastly, the performance evaluation session can help to support personal accountability and provide a basis for financially rewarding employees.

Although many people experience some anxiety during the performance review session, the benefits generally outweigh the time and effort. The performance evaluation session can provide an opportunity for documenting the employee's performance and serve as a system of fairness by informing employees how well they are performing in the organization.

There are many types of performance evaluation systems, such as narrative appraisals, formative and summative assessments, 360, rating systems, and goal-based evaluations. Some organizations utilize an *open narrative evaluation*, especially for high-level administrators and managers. In this system the subordinate is asked to write a narrative regarding how well he or she performed during the year. This narrative is then used as a basis for a performance review session. This type of system is more of an informal approach and is infrequently used.

The *formative assessment* is often used to support the summative evaluation process. During the formative assessment, ongoing informal feedback is given to the employee by the supervisor, and this information is not used as part of the employee's permanent evaluation record. The whole idea of formative assessment is to give informal feedback without the fear of the information negatively affecting the employee's performance. However, it is sometimes difficult to entirely disregard the information when preparing a summative report.

The *summative evaluation* is a popular approach and consists of a combination of a rating assessment and narrative section for adding comments on the evaluation form. It is typically conducted once a year for an employee. The evaluation form can consist of a paper copy and be filed in a cabinet or an electronic copy and be stored in a computer. The *360 performance evaluation* is a system that uses a multi-rater feedback process to obtain an evaluation on an employee.

The 360 feedback is often provided by multiple supervisors, peers, support staff, community members, and possibly students. This system began during the 1950s in the corporate world and gradually gained popularity among human resources professionals. However, the system has been somewhat controversial in that it requires extensive time to collect the feedback and some people feel that the information is not always accurate or used exclusively for developmental purposes.

The traditional *combination rating* and *open-comment evaluation* is still probably the most popular rating form. The evaluation of an employee is generally conducted on a semiannual or annual basis. Non-tenured teachers are generally evaluated on a semiannual basis and tenured teachers evaluated annually.

Conducting evaluations on an ongoing basis provides a good opportunity to obtain regular feedback, although this can be time consuming for both the teacher and teacher evaluator. Typically, the annual review is the requirement by school districts and state departments of education. Also the use of computer software has greatly increased the efficiency in completing and storing the evaluation forms into one database.

Regardless of the performance evaluation system used, there can be many problems associated with conducting the evaluation session (see Figure 6.3). One problem is having sufficient time to prepare the form and complete the review session. Conducting a shallow evaluation with a teacher not only shows indifference but may demotivate the teacher.

The *leniency effect* occurs when teacher evaluators rate teachers too high in all the performance factors. This may happen when the teacher evaluators desire to avoid dealing with potential teacher dissatisfaction or resistance. Teacher evaluators may also overrate teachers to avoid creating conflict with them. *Central tendency* occurs when the teacher evaluator rates all the performance factors in the middle of the scale. This might indicate that the teacher evaluator is indecisive and can't make a decision.

One of the most difficult aspects in completing a performance evaluation is to ensure that all teacher evaluators strive to have a common understanding of what constitutes the performance standards of a

add this to observation narrative

1. Poor preparation, hasty review, or not taking the review seriously
2. Leniency effect
3. Central tendency rating
4. Recency effect rating
5. Poor inter-rater reliability
6. Personal prejudice and bias or being too confrontational or directive
7. Game playing or manipulating the performance system
8. Rater indecisiveness
9. Being overly judgmental or emotional
10. Conducting a shallow performance evaluation review

Figure 6.3.   Problems in Conducting Performance Evaluations

teacher, a term called *inter-rater reliability.* It is generally advisable that all teacher evaluators participate in performance evaluation training to understand the criteria for rating employees and different levels of *standards of performance.*

Another problem with rating teachers involves the human effect of *harboring prejudice or bias* toward a person, which may influence the rating. Although the performance evaluation should be conducted objectively, it is nearly impossible to exclude personal subjectivity. *Game playing* is another problem with performance evaluations, which occurs when a teacher evaluator over- or underrates an employee to support organizational politics.

For example, if a new teacher is being rated during the first six months, the teacher evaluator may rate the new teacher lower to help protect himself or herself later should he or she desire to terminate the new teacher for cause or deny the teacher tenure. The teacher leader may also rate a teacher lower to allow the teacher *room to grow.* All these examples are *game playing* and should be avoided.

The teacher evaluator also should avoid being too judgmental, emotional, directive, or controlling during the performance evaluation session. Other problems associated with conducting a performance evaluation include:

- Rating a teacher based upon personal characteristics that violate discrimination laws
- Telling the teacher about the rating or performance of other teachers in the organization
- Changing a rating during the teacher session because of undue pressure by the teacher
- Conducting the session in a non-private location
- Focusing the appraisal review session on the teacher evaluator's performance rather than largely on the teacher's
- Giving false promises to a teacher to avoid conflict with the teacher
- Rating the teacher exceptionally high in an effort to gain the teacher's favor and support
- Rating the teacher low with the ulterior purpose of withholding a pay raise
- Overweighting of recent occurrences that are either favorable or unfavorable and omitting past performance

Most performance evaluation forms contain *performance rating levels* and *definitions.* For example, it is common to have *a five-level rating system* ranging from unacceptable to exceptional, which is similar to a rating scale used by Oklahoma and New Mexico. Some forms have a three-rating level system consisting of not satisfactory, satisfactory, and outstanding, which is similar to that used by the states of North Carolina, Kansas, and Kentucky.

The Danielson *Framework for Teaching* model uses a rubric with four performance levels called unsatisfactory, needs improvement, meets performance, and exceeds performance (Danielson, 2007). Most states use a four-level rating system. The Danielson model also outlines strategies on using the model for recruiting teachers, mentoring and induction, peer coaching, supervision, and evaluation. Use the performance evaluation form that has been approved by the district and state department of education.

Also, many states in the United States have passed legislation outlining guidelines and requirements on teacher evaluation. For example, the State of Oregon passed legislation in 2012 that requires specific elements in evaluating teachers and administrators. These elements consist of standards of professional practice, differentiated levels, multiple measures, evaluation and professional growth cycle, and alignment with professional learning (Oregon Department of Education, 2012).

Figure 6.4 lists the typical steps for conducting the annual performance session. Every school district should provide sufficient training and guidelines in conducting the performance evaluation for all teacher evaluators. Step one, the *preparation for the performance evaluation session*, should be thorough. It is important to schedule sufficient time and choose a location that is private and without distractions.

Generally it is advisable for the teacher to complete a self-reflection prior to the session. This gives the teacher ample time to participate in self-reflection on his or performance for the year. The advantage of sending the self-assessment in advance allows the teacher leader to anticipate the teacher's evaluation although it might bias the teacher evaluator's own rating of the team member.

In step two, the teacher evaluator *introduces the session* by providing an overview for the process and establishing expectations and criteria for ratings, and essentially sets the stage for the performance appraisal session. The third step involves the teacher evaluator *reviewing all the performance ratings* for all the sections on the form. Generally, a teacher evaluator reviews each of the ratings and then gives an *overall rating* at the end in step four.

However, it is possible that the teacher evaluator may want to give the overall rating prior to reviewing each of the rating sections. This might be the case when there is an outstanding teacher and giving the overall rating in advance may help to reduce anxiety and allow for a more constructive discussion. When evaluating a poor performer it is advisable to give

Step 1	• Prepare the performance evaluation form
Step 2	• Introduce the performance evaluation session
Step 3	• Review the performance evaluation ratings
Step 4	• State the performance evaluation rating
Step 5	• Discuss performance developmental areas
Step 6	• Obtain the teacher's signature on the form
Step 7	• Agree on goals and professional growth plan
Step 8	• Document and file evaluation form

Figure 6.4. Steps in Conducting a Summative Performance Evaluation Session

the overall rating at the end so the teacher evaluator can build justification for the rating, especially if the employee needs to be placed on probation.

After the rating has been given it is often good to obtain the *teacher's overall reaction* and then discuss general *development areas,* step five. It is critical to *obtain the signature* of the teacher on the performance appraisal form, step six. The signature does not indicate that the teacher agrees to the form but acknowledges that the form has been reviewed with the teacher.

Also an optional step in the summative session might be for the teacher evaluator to *discuss next year's goals* and agree upon the goals with the teacher, step 7. In this case the teacher evaluator may request that the teacher prepare in advance and bring these goals to the session. This approach can help expedite the process and avoid the need for another meeting.

The summative performance evaluation session concludes by *documenting and filing all forms* in accordance with district policy, step eight. In the event that follow-up is needed for teachers who may be placed on probation, a schedule would be developed. Also it is important that the forms be sealed and held confidential to protect the employee and institution.

REMEDIATION AND PROFESSIONAL GROWTH PLANS

For teachers who are performing less than satisfactorily, most states require a remediation program consisting of coaching and the establishment of a *performance improvement plan.* Research has shown that up to one-third of new teachers leave a school district within three years (National Center for Educational Statistics, 2012). Therefore, school districts need to provide a meaningful teacher coaching performance development system to help support all teachers, especially for those who are not performing to acceptable standards.

Once it has been determined that a teacher is not performing to acceptable standards, remediation is required by most states. The remediation process generally consists of a teacher evaluator developing a performance improvement plan in collaboration with the teacher. This plan then becomes part of the formal, official record of performance.

Most all *remediation performance improvement plans* require the teacher to eventually perform at a satisfactory level, within a prescribed time frame, or the teacher may be terminated. Many states require that the teacher evaluator complete and pass state training to be qualified to provide performance coaching and monitor the performance improvement plan.

The basic steps for conducting remediation coaching, as described in chapter 3, generally include teacher observation consisting of a *pre-conference, observation, analysis,* and *post-conference feedback.* During the pre-conference discussion, the mentor schedules the time and place for observation in collaboration with the teacher. Teacher evaluators should utilize the district's *teaching framework model,* which generally includes observing teachers throughout the entire observation process.

The district teaching framework model should be a research-based instructional guideline that links teaching responsibilities and activities together that can be measured. For example, the Danielson model encompasses four domains: planning and preparation, classroom environment, instruction, and professional responsibilities (Danielson, 2007).

When assessing teachers, based upon a framework for teaching, a rubric should always be used. The rubric describes various levels of performance such as unsatisfactory, needs improvement, meets performance, and exceeds performance. There are several types of rubrics and evaluation scales, and teacher leaders should use them consistently within the district.

add to narrative

During the observation, the teacher evaluator should record and evaluate teachers on all aspects of teaching and classroom management. Afterward, a careful analysis and review of the information should be completed in preparation for the post-conference meeting. During this meeting the teacher leader mentor should give constructive feedback to the teacher.

The teacher evaluator should regularly provide casual feedback by asking questions such as "Describe things that are going well for you," "Describe some areas that you would like to improve," "What things can I do as a teacher evaluator to better assist you?" The feedback given to teachers and staff members, in addition to being a formative process, can also be summative.

Providing *effective coaching* for all teachers, whether new or experienced, is a major responsibility of teacher leaders. All teacher leaders should be well trained in providing coaching for teachers and staff. Examples of coaching topics include instruction and curriculum, classroom management, handling discipline, using instructional technology, and administrative requirements. Figure 6.5 lists steps in conducting a coaching session.

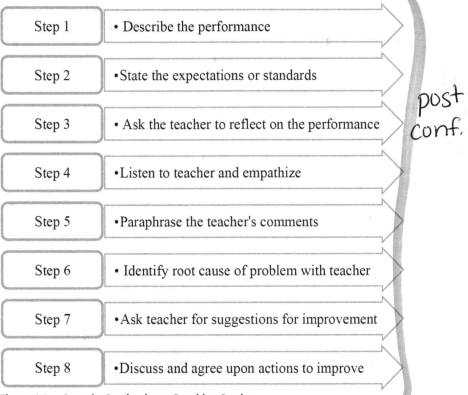

post conf.

Step 1	• Describe the performance
Step 2	• State the expectations or standards
Step 3	• Ask the teacher to reflect on the performance
Step 4	• Listen to teacher and empathize
Step 5	• Paraphrase the teacher's comments
Step 6	• Identify root cause of problem with teacher
Step 7	• Ask teacher for suggestions for improvement
Step 8	• Discuss and agree upon actions to improve

Figure 6.5.   Steps in Conducting a Coaching Session

During the first step of the coaching session, the teacher evaluator should *describe the performance* of the new teacher. During this stage, the teacher evaluator begins by humanizing the setting and being objective and direct in describing performance that needs to be improved. For example, issues might include the need for improved instruction, handling of a student disciplinary case, or improving lesson plans.

Step two requires the teacher evaluator to describe the *desired expectation* or standard. For example, the teacher leader may state that lesson plans need to be error free and well organized and need to contain all components outlined in the school policy manual. Examples may be given to the teacher to show the desired expectation.

Step three involves the teacher *reflecting upon his or her performance* and identifying positive behaviors and areas in need of improvement. This reflection can be a valuable method to help a teacher examine his or her performance without the teacher leader directly stating the problem. For example, the teacher may conclude that he or she is having difficulty handling student misbehavior and needs to better administer the school district policies.

An important step in the coaching session is for the teacher evaluator to *sincerely listen* and *empathize* with his or her feelings, step four. The use of paraphrasing in step five also helps to verify what the teacher stated and confirm mutual understanding. Typical statements might be "I can understand how you feel in a situation like this," "I can see how someone would have these feelings in a situation like this" or "I was once a new teacher as well and understand."

Paraphrasing also can help to show that the teacher leader is demonstrating active listening and helps in personalizing the conversation and developing an atmosphere of respect. In addition, paraphrasing ensures understanding of the message being communicated, and this technique can be helpful for both the teacher evaluator and teacher.

Step six involves the teacher *identifying the root cause* of the performance problem. This step is similar to step three but goes into greater detail. For example, if a teacher is experiencing difficulty in handling disciplinary problems, the potential root causes might include distractions from outside influences, health issues, a poor attitude, need for additional training, or a dysfunctional school environment. It is important for the teacher leader to reinforce the teacher's responsibility for improvement and to provide encouragement for improvement.

The seventh step entails *asking the teacher for solutions* for the performance issue. In this way, the teacher is more likely to accept the solution. It also allows the new teacher to take responsibility for his or her own behavior. For example, the teacher may need to include more engaging instructional activities or learn to control to his or her emotions when dealing with student misbehavior.

In step eight, the teacher evaluator and teacher should *discuss and agree upon an action plan* for resolving the performance issue. There may be some negotiation so they can collaboratively resolve the issue. The teacher should propose a solution that is acceptable to the teacher evaluator because he or she will be more apt to accept the solution rather than its being imposed upon him or her. However, if the teacher's suggestion is unacceptable to the teacher evaluator, further discussion may be necessary, and ultimately they will need to mutually arrive at an effective action.

The session ends with the teacher evaluator thanking the teacher for participating in the coaching session and building his or her confidence. Building the confidence of a teacher has reinforcing consequences. It also may be worthwhile to schedule a follow-up session to review progress of the teacher's performance.

Even if a teacher evaluator has difficulty in supporting a teacher, especially because of very poor performance incidents, the teacher evaluator needs to continue to maintain a positive working relationship. Otherwise, the coach–teacher relationship will be undermined, and the teacher may resort to retaliatory actions that become stressful and time consuming.

During the coaching process, the teacher evaluator also should be aware of his or her subtle, non-verbal cues, which the teacher may observe, that are incongruent with the teacher leader's verbal message, for example, stating something positive to the teacher but coming across with defensive body language. The teacher evaluator may also suggest a follow-up session to review the teacher's progress.

STATE AND FEDERAL LAWS AFFECTING COACHING AND EVALUATIONS

add to post conf.

Critical to the performance evaluation session is adhering to federal, state, and school district laws and policies. There are several laws and potential union contract agreements that need to be understood by teacher leaders before administering the performance appraisal session. Besides teachers, all employees need to understand these laws, and a copy of them should be displayed on the institution's bulletin board and website.

Most federal laws include additions to the *Civil Rights Act of 1964*, which prohibits against discrimination on the basis of race, sex, religion, national origin, color, and certain medical conditions. The teacher evaluator should make sure to refrain from noting any performance that reference any of these factors that could be construed as discriminatory (Tomal and Schilling, 2014).

For example, a teacher coach should not rate a female employee lower just because she is pregnant. Another law that may affect the appraisal is the *Age Discrimination Act of 1967*, which prohibits age discrimination beginning at age forty. A teacher leader should avoid comments such as "Nice job for an old man," or "You need to get with it and get out of the Dark Ages and learn technology like the young teachers."

Negative comments based on age can not only be hurtful to an employee but also potentially illegal and a violation of the institution's values and code of conduct. Also statements regarding people's lifestyle if irrelevant to the employee's performance or institution's codes of conduct should be avoided. There is difficulty in discerning actual age discrimination, and local school counsel should always be consulted.

Another law that may affect a performance evaluation session is the *Americans with Disabilities Act of 1990*, which prohibits discrimination on the basis of actual, previous, or perceived mental or physical disability. A teacher evaluator should demonstrate caution in rating a disabled employee if reasonable accommodations have not been provided that could have improved his or her performance.

The *Title VII, Section 1604, Sexual Harassment Law* may also apply during the performance appraisal session. A teacher evaluator may genuinely express concern for an employee and may want to show support by giving the employee a hug or by embracing the employee during a coaching or evaluation session. The teacher evaluator should restrain from touching the employee in any manner other than perhaps a handshake.

Although the teacher evaluator may have good intentions, these types of actions may be construed to be sexual harassment behaviors and should be avoided. The teacher evaluator should be careful in the choice of words and avoid terms such as "honey," "cutie," "good girl," "you're a good boy," or other gender-based statements that could be somewhat belittling and disrespectful and potentially violate sexual harassment laws.

Another federal law that may affect the evaluation session is the *Family Medical Leave Act of 1993*. This law prohibits discrimination against employees who request time off for their own serious illness or that of a family member. This law may have implications in giving a performance rating to an employee, especially if the rating is less than satisfactory when the performance issue might have been because of an approved leave of absence by the employee. These types of performance issues are not always clear cut and demand careful thought by the teacher coach.

Other potential problems may be affected by union agreement. For example, a contractual agreement may allow an employee to request a third party to be present during an evaluation session, especially when the evaluation is anticipated to be unfavorable to the employee.

SUMMARY

The proper establishment of a teacher evaluation system requires a systematic and comprehensive knowledge of human resource management. Understanding the myriad of state and federal laws and local school policies is critical in designing teacher evaluation forms and assessments, and effectively evaluating teachers. The proper mentoring and coaching of teachers who need remediation is also an important component of the teacher evaluation process and contributes to high morale in the organization.

Moreover, conducting effective performance evaluations can help ensure that teachers perform to the standards required in the *school improvement plan*. This will help to support the vision and key strategies of the school district. A collaborative approach to the supervision and improvement of learning also can help to ensure agreement and success in producing high-performing team members.

CASE STUDY

You recently have been been promoted as a team member on the *teacher evaluation task force* at the Kennedy School District 103. The school superintendent has asked your team to prepare a comprehensive proposal for improving the teacher evaluation process, which supports state policies and guidelines. He has also asked that the plan be a collaborative one that does not hinder overall teacher morale and motivation. Prepare a two- to three-page action plan for achieving this request.

EXERCISES AND DISCUSSION QUESTIONS

1. Describe several examples of policies that states connect to teacher evaluations, and in your opinion, which ones are most effective in evaluating teachers?
2. List and describe some of the relevant federal, state, and school laws and policies affecting the evaluation of teachers.
3. List the characteristics of an effective teacher evaluation system.
4. Describe some major steps in providing remedial coaching to a teacher.

REFERENCES

Danielson, C. (2007). *Enhancing professional practice: A framework for teaching*. Alexandria, VA: Association for Supervision and Curriculum Development.

National Center for Educational Statistics. (2012). http://nces.ed.gov/

National Council on Teacher Quality. (2013). *Connecting the dots: Using evaluations of teacher effectiveness to inform policy and practice*. http://www.nctq.org

Ohio Teacher Evaluation System. (2011). http://www.education.ohio.gov

Oregon Department of Education. (2012). http://www.ode.state.or.us

Performance Evaluation Reform Act (PERA). (2010). Education Reform in Illinois. www.isbe.state.il.us/PERA/default.htm

Tomal, D., & Schilling, C. (2013). *Managing human resources and collective bargaining*. Lanham, MD: Rowman & Littlefield Education, Inc.

7

+

A Professional Learning and Growth Expedition

OBJECTIVES

At the conclusion of this chapter you will be able to:

1. Understand the central role of values, mission, and vision in fostering school improvement and professional learning and growth for teachers (ELCC 1.3, 1.4; ISLLC 1, 2; TLEC 3; InTASC 9; Learning Forward Standards).
2. Examine school-related data as part of planning for professional learning and growth (ELCC 2.4; ISLLC 1, 2, 3, 4; TLEC 2, 4, 5; InTASC 2, 6; Learning Forward Standards).
3. Describe strategies utilized by leaders to prioritize, implement, monitor, and evaluate professional learning and growth of teachers (ELCC 2.1, 3.3, 5.1, 5.2, 5.3; ISLLC 1, 2, 3, 4, 5; TLEC 1, 2, 3, 4, 5, 6; InTASC 3, 4, 5, 6, 7, 9, 10; Learning Forward Standards).

THE EXPEDITION

An expedition typically refers to a trip undertaken for a specific purpose. The trip we invite you to undertake in this final chapter leads to a specific purpose: professional learning and growth for the teachers and leaders in your school. Similar to an expedition, planning, execution, and judgment regarding the progress of your journey is necessary.

As the leader, you will assemble a group of people demonstrating individual talents who you believe will work as a team until the end of the journey. The expedition will involve consultation and planning with others before and during the trip as well as the gathering and utilizing of resources.

The journey will be lengthy, and at times, the terrain will be tough. Some planned and unplanned events will occur based on external and internal conditions in your school. The expedition will take endurance and address many realities that you encounter along the way. The steps in the journey should be measured and evaluated to ensure that the purpose is met, and plans or implementation may need to be adjusted or abandoned.

With the metaphor of an expedition in mind, let's examine the typical steps of the expedition that school leaders undertake when they engage in developing *professional learning and growth plans* for teachers. The reason for the journey is to improve learning for all students, which requires learning and growth of teachers. It is understood that sometimes the sequence may be altered, but rarely is any step deleted.

In chapters 4 and 5, three levels of professional development—district level, school level, and individual level—were explained and illustrated. In this chapter, we will follow one expedition at the middle school level. In doing so, we will see how professional learning and growth can be undertaken when it is aligned and integrated at all three levels.

SETTING THE COURSE

Figure 7.1 identifies the steps in the expedition. This chapter will examine eight major steps that are guided by the leader to develop a professional learning and growth plan for a school. Examples and illustrations will accompany the steps to offer samples and models for your use.

The first step in the expedition is to *examine the values, mission, and vision of the school as* discussed in chapter 1. Sometimes leaders begin with part of step two, focusing on student needs, without considering the mission of the school or its *capacity, skills, knowledge,* and *disposition* to carry out its responsibilities. At other times, leaders begin with ambitious goal setting, which is really the third step in the process. Instead, a thorough consideration of the values, mission, and vision of the school is needed to guide our journey.

The *values* are the guiding principles of the school and represent the attitudes that the community says are important. Some people define values as the underlying philosophy of an organization, while others state that it is the philosophy that underpins decisions. In all cases, the values

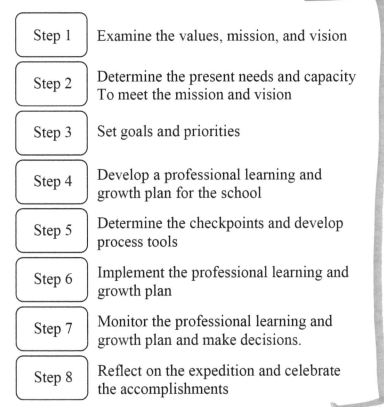

Step 1	Examine the values, mission, and vision
Step 2	Determine the present needs and capacity To meet the mission and vision
Step 3	Set goals and priorities
Step 4	Develop a professional learning and growth plan for the school
Step 5	Determine the checkpoints and develop process tools
Step 6	Implement the professional learning and growth plan
Step 7	Monitor the professional learning and growth plan and make decisions.
Step 8	Reflect on the expedition and celebrate the accomplishments

Figure 7.1. Steps in Developing a Professional Learning and Growth Plan for a School

are influential in setting the direction of the school. See Figure 7.2 for an example of a school values statement.

The *mission statement* is the written declaration of the purpose of the school. Instructional decisions made by the leader should be in alignment with it. The mission states why your school exists and what it prepares the student to do each day. Fostering the optimal level of support and incentives to enhance professional learning and growth is an essential role of instructional leaders. The values, mission, and vision of the school should govern which needs and goals are selected and prioritized for teacher learning.

For example, if the mission states that the organization provides a learner-centered environment so each student reaches his or her potential, then the priorities for teacher learning and growth should be aligned. For a teacher, this would include determining specific goals for each student based on the student's individual potential.

School Values Statement

Student Focus: Provide quality educational services to our students in a caring environment with continual focus on improvement.

Leadership: Demonstrate servant leadership as we work with stakeholders.

Quality and Excellence: Strive for excellence in all our undertakings.

Ethics: Maintain high integrity, ethics and professionalism.

Innovation: Expand our capacities and utilize advanced technologies to meet ever-changing needs of our students.

Diversity: Demonstrate respect for diverse cultures and traditions of our community.

Collaboration: Foster teamwork and collaboration between and among our students, parents and community.

start here

Figure 7.2.   Example of a School Values Statement

Also, teacher learning and growth priorities would emphasize the development of an array of strategies that are learner, not teacher, centered. A plan to assist teachers to improve reading performance in line with the mission, therefore, would need to include both of these skill sets, targeting goals and using learner-centered strategies.

Similarly, the *vision statement* provides an inspiring visualization of your school in the future. It influences many of the midterm and long-term goals of your organization including teacher learning and growth. If the *vision* of the school is to prepare a student to become a lifelong problem solver and adapt to the changes of the twenty-first century, teacher learning would be affected. Emphasis on how to develop student tasks that require unraveling problems, facing challenges, proposing solutions, and assessing progress would need to be part of the instructional strategies of every teacher.

The use of a wide array of technological resources to locate and evaluate reputable information in relation to the problem would be needed. Both student and teacher would need to possess these skill sets. Organizing and presenting one's findings based on the research conducted would be necessary. All of these resources would become essential in that school for a teacher as part of professional learning and growth.

Without the values, mission, and vision of a school uppermost in the leader's mind, instructional changes become a series of recent trends or fads based on what others are doing or as reported in the media or at conferences. A popular, new strategy should not drive professional growth. Similarly, the comfort level of teachers with the present goals and strategies that do not meet student needs should not prevent teacher learning. Instead, it is the leader's responsibility to clarify how what was done in the past is not working, and how what is being advocated for change in professional goals ties directly to the mission and vision of the school. Then the role and responsibilities of each teacher should be outlined. This helps to make clear what every member is expected to do.

If your school does not have a values, mission, and vision statement, or if it has not been reviewed and renewed in the past five years, this task should be undertaken before your next plan for teacher learning and growth is developed. Some schools develop or review their *values, mission, and vision statement* in conjunction with the development of their *strategic plan*, while others develop it at a separate time.

A *strategic plan* involves representative stakeholders visualizing the desired future for the school and transforming the vision into broadly stated goals. Teachers, school leaders, parents, community members, and students are stakeholders who serve on a strategic planning committee due to their vested interest in seeing that the school serves the expectations of each group. The strategic plan utilizes the values, mission, and vision statement to set direction.

Figure 7.3 traces the process of developing *values, mission, and vision statements*. At the end, each group should see that it has made an important contribution, and the final form should be embraced by all. The statements, taken together, should drive teaching and learning on a daily basis.

The role of the leader after development of the values, mission, and vision statements includes communicating them, applying them, and monitoring them. The statements should be prominently displayed in written communications and visible throughout the school. Effective leaders make reference to both often, and together they serve as a compass in focusing attention on the reasons decisions are made.

The second step in the expedition is to *determine the present needs and capacity to meet the mission and vision* of the school (see Figure 7.1). *Needs*

Seek an expert facilitator from outside the school
and community to assist with objectivity

Make sure all representative stakeholders are
represented so the statements are owned by the
group in their final form

Designate responsibilities so each representative
group sees the importance of its contributions

Develop the statements

Revise by substituting key terms until the
statements are as precise as possible in
communicating the present purpose and future
image of the school

Figure 7.3.   Values, Mission, and Vision Statement Development Process

are the essential requisites for teaching and learning. *Capacity* is the ability to perform the roles and responsibilities one is given. Both new and veteran leaders should begin to ascertain the present needs of the school with an examination of *student-related data*. The leader should not engage in this activity alone. Depending on the size of the school, teachers or a group of teacher representatives should be convened.

In some schools, an administrator leads the team as it considers relevant information, while in other districts, individuals and groups investigate separately and bring their findings to a meeting. The focus of all individuals and groups is the same: What evidence do we have that students are learning and meeting the mission and vision of the school?

Two purposes are served when evidence must be brought forth in making claims that students are learning. First, the strengths and needs of the students are revealed and discussed in relation to the mission of the school. Second, the leader gathers important information about the *capacity* of the teachers in relation to student needs. DuFour (2014) and others confirm that these two areas lead to the best kind of professional learning and growth for school improvement.

Understanding how the teachers conduct their analyses reveals important information about their knowledge, skills, and attitudes. What processes are used as they analyze information? Any shortcomings noted should be added to the plan for professional learning and growth in the third step, setting goals and priorities.

Figure 7.4 illustrates the types of *student-related data* that should be considered by the leader and faculty representatives in determining needs. Student-related data assist teachers and leaders in focusing on factors that measure or may affect student learning. There are many types of data available in a school that may be used.

Investigating student performance, school climate, demographics, finance and operations, and teacher performance will provide specific details about the present composition of the school and how resources are allocated. Comparing single examples of data types to data compiled *longitudinally*, using three points such as the beginning, middle, and end of the year or over a three-year span at the same time each year, will assist in seeing patterns or trends that should be considered as professional learning and growth is planned.

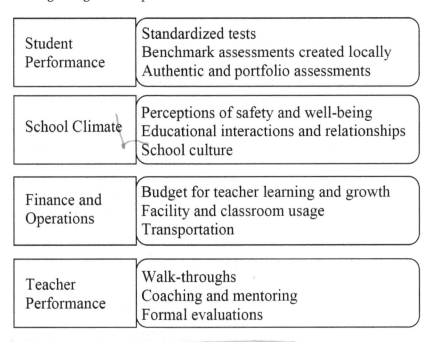

Student Performance	Standardized tests Benchmark assessments created locally Authentic and portfolio assessments
School Climate	Perceptions of safety and well-being Educational interactions and relationships School culture
Finance and Operations	Budget for teacher learning and growth Facility and classroom usage Transportation
Teacher Performance	Walk-throughs Coaching and mentoring Formal evaluations

Figure 7.4. Examples of Types of School Data to Examine

Student Performance

By examining student performance, important student outcomes can be measured. Results of standardized tests, locally prepared benchmark assessments, and portfolios of student work are among the most frequently appraised types of information. Faculty team members and leaders engaging in this type of analysis should possess basic understanding of statistical terms, ability to organize information to reveal patterns and longitudinal trends, and a thorough knowledge of the standards upon which the assessments are based.

School Climate

An examination of school climate is another set of data that should be explored by the leader and leadership team members. Some schools invite the students, parents, teachers, and leaders to complete surveys annually or periodically to garner perceptions. *The National School Climate Center,* formerly known as the *Center for Social and Emotional Education,* offers five dimensions (safety, teaching and learning, interpersonal relationships, institutional environment, and teacher relationships) that should be included in any survey.

Related features such as rules and norms, sense of personal security, sense of social-emotional security, and support for learning are assessed. Four other areas including social support for adults, social support for students, school connectedness or engagement, and leadership professional relationships are included in their surveys.

For those wishing to consider a survey or find one that may be better suited to the dimensions and features of your school, *A School Climate Survey Compendia* is available through the *National Center for Safe Supportive Learning Environments* (2014) as an online warehouse to examine surveys already available, and continual additions are made to it.

Surveys developed by non-federal and federal groups and some states including Alaska, California, and Arizona may be viewed for consideration, too. You may prefer to create one of your own using features most related to the five dimensions or customized based on your mission. Figure 7.5 illustrates a partial sample of a school climate survey.

One of the most crucial components for a leader to measure about school climate is *school culture.* In addition to items on the school climate survey relating to teacher perceptions of school culture, leaders should add observations and interactions in the school that the leader has personally witnessed along with visible signs of the culture.

School culture assessment focuses on the shared beliefs, attitudes, actions, and values that teachers and leaders hold for meeting the

Name of School: _____

Directions: Please indicate your group by circling it and then answer the following
             questions.

   Group #1: Grades 1–3   Group #2: Grades 4–5   Group #3: Grades 6–8

Using the scale below, circle the extent of your agreement with each statement.

5	4	3	2	1
Strongly Agree	Agree	Undecided	Disagree	Strongly Disagree

1. I feel safe when I am in school.	5 4 3 2 1
2. School policies in the student handbook are clearly stated and followed.	5 4 3 2 1
3. Teachers use a variety of strategies to help students learn.	5 4 3 2 1
4. Teachers know the individual strengths and challenges of students.	5 4 3 2 1
5. I am respected by students, teachers, and administrators in the school.	5 4 3 2 1
6. The individuals in the school know how to resolve their differences.	5 4 3 2 1
7. The school building and rooms are utilized to promote student learning.	5 4 3 2 1
8. Adequate resources are available to students and teachers.	5 4 3 2 1
9. Adults in the building work together to meet the needs of students.	5 4 3 2 1
10. Teachers are consulted before changes are made which affect them.	5 4 3 2 1

Sample open-ended questions

  1. What are the best qualities of our school?

  2. How could we improve our school? State your specific suggestions.

Figure 7.5. Partial Copy of a School Climate Survey

school-related needs of all of its members and confronting the difficulties
it faces. Statements, actions, and physical manifestations of teachers and
leaders are of prime concern.

How teachers and leaders honor their accomplishments and confront
challenging students and situations reveals aspects of their *capacity.*
Teacher attitudes and resilience may need to be developed as part of the
teacher learning and growth plan. Figure 7.6 includes sample questions
that a leader should ask to assess *school culture.*

The Three "A"s of School Culture
Leaders Should Ask These Questions

Accomplishments	*Attitudes*	*Approaches*

		- What resources are available and how do they secure assistance when needed?
- What do staff and students consider their proudest achievements?	- Is there an attitude of "can do" on the part of teachers and students?	- Are a number of different strategies used when the first one does not succeed?
- What signs of success are posted in the classrooms and halls?	- Can teachers and students offer examples of when they have triumphed in the face of defeat or did not reach their goals and reflected on what to do better?	- Do teachers and students work singly or in groups to solve problems?
- Which triumphs have been shared with others and in what form?		

Figure 7.6. Questions to Assess the Three "A"s of School Culture

When an administration enumerates its accomplishments in an annual report to the school board or on its website, and the teachers report the same milestones in faculty meetings, a leader begins to see evidence that elements of a shared culture exist. Frequent newsletters to parents by teachers and news updates to the community by the administration sharing similar information is another positive signal.

When grade level, department, school, and community meetings include recognitions and celebrations about these same milestones, another tangible sign is apparent. Banners, e-mails, and tweets to constituencies, and press releases announcing these landmarks signal a positive sign of a visible, constructive school culture. The absence of most of these should cause concern and indicate attention is necessary on the part of the leader to incorporate these tangible indicators.

The attitude and approach the group as a whole has toward change and challenge is another sign of school culture. A *positive culture* understands that the needs of the students and teachers will change over time because people, the society, and the knowledge in the disciplines change over time such as technology. A *positive culture* views change as part of the process in responding to the needs of the students.

Although challenges occur from political, economic, and social arenas, a *positive culture* feels it has the capacity to meet the demands and develop appropriate responses and solutions. When the *school culture* is consistently *negative* and teachers feel overwhelmed with the problems they face, plans for building teachers' skills and confidence should be added to professional learning and growth plans.

Demographics

Examination of *demographic* data can provide important information about students, which should be considered in planning teacher learning. The current age, gender, ethnicity, socioeconomic status, and student mobility should be considered. Often, what are equally revealing are the trends in the school over the past three to ten years and information provided by the census or community sources.

Table 7.1 is a sample of demographic information that a school could examine to find trends in enrollment over a five-year period especially in the areas of those eligible for *Free or Reduced Lunch* and English Language Learners (ELL) services. Reports by housing agencies, religious organizations, and local government assist faculty in preparing for and responding to changing student populations.

Table 7.1. Example of Demographic Trends: 2010 and 2014

	October 2010	*October 2014*
Total # of Students	1,578	1,639
Free or Reduced Lunch %	35.3	43.9
English Language Learners %	8.7	13.3
Special Education Learners %	13.5	14.1
Ethnicity		
Total # of Students	1,578	1,639
American Indian or Alaskan Native	0	0
Asian or Pacific Islander	551	599
Black, Non-Hispanic	177	175
Hispanic	150	152
White, Non-Hispanic	672	592
Multiracial	28	121

Finance and Operations

By examining data in the areas of finance and operations, information regarding available resources for new programs and professional learning may be ascertained. Usage of rooms and space during each period during the school day, as well as before and after school, can be noted. Availability of transportation services might be necessary to offer a program for a group of students with similar needs across a number of school buildings.

Figure 7.7 illustrates how a budget for professional learning and growth had been allocated for a three-year period. When decisions are being made by the team for future professional learning, reallocations across the five categories might be necessary to reach the targeted goals.

There is a growing trend to consider alternatives to salary scale lane advancement as the primary manner in which incentives for teachers are offered. For example, if the mission of the district includes that students will be proficient in the use of technology for college and career readiness,

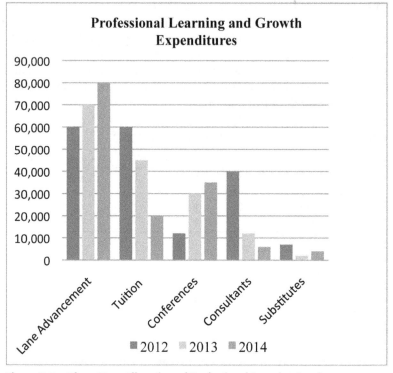

Figure 7.7.   **Three-Year Allocation of Professional Learning Funds**

the earning of advanced degrees or endorsements in that field by teachers may be enhanced by transferring resources to tuition.

The encouragement by the district of faculty who wish to work closely with other colleagues and become teacher leaders could be promoted by allocating incentives from salary scale lane advancement to accepting leadership roles in the school that are non-administrative. Union contracts may need to be renegotiated, but when a team and faculty understand the skill sets needed for continual improvement, reallocation of funds create a win-win scenario for all.

Creativity is necessary to allocate and use funds wisely. Sometimes two or more districts can pool resources to stretch dollars. Funding an expensive keynote speaker or conference may be accomplished by advertising and charging fees to those outside the district. Grant funds may be available, especially through businesses or local community members who have been invited as partners to develop the talents and interests of students and teachers in exchange for service in the community.

Teacher Performance

By examining teacher performance data in relation to student needs, information can be gathered for deciding about goals for professional learning and growth of teachers. Some of the data may be available only to school leaders such as percentages of teachers at each of the four- or five level rating scales within a school district as discussed in chapter 6.

Other data may have been collected during walk-throughs and peer coaching sessions by both teachers and school leaders and could be examined to reveal patterns of usage across the school. Figure 7.8 is an example of a summary of strategies observed across grades K–12 in one school district. Combining information collected only by evaluators with figures collected by the teachers can assist decision-making regarding needed teacher growth areas.

Some of the needs of the school will emanate from policies and mandates outside the school. Private institutions may be governed by a constituent group, charter, or religious organization, while many schools are regulated when they choose to take federal funds. For example, Title III funds for English Language Learners (ELLs) require schools to offer specific kinds of programs and hire teachers with certain qualifications.

Meeting these requirements involves strengthening the preparation of ELL teachers and all teachers in a school so that they may organize and deliver content using strategies that will be effective for students. The required mandates for program staffing and delivery become part of planning efforts when selecting targets for professional learning and growth activities.

Grade Levels	Total # Observations	Strategies Incorporated	# Seen*
K–2	72	Generating and Testing Hypotheses	6
		Using Non-Linguistic Representations	23
		Summarizing	4
		Using Cooperative Learning	12
		Lecturing and Modeling	37
3–5	68	Generating and Testing Hypotheses	12
		Using Non-Linguistic Representations	18
		Summarizing	26
		Cooperative Learning	35
		Lecture/Model	28
6–8	78	Generating and Testing Hypotheses	17
		Using Non-Linguistic Representations	9
		Summarizing	49
		Cooperative Learning	44
		Lecture/Model	50
9–12	107	Generating and Testing Hypotheses	16
		Using Non-Linguistic Representations	12
		Summarizing	14
		Cooperative Learning	46
		Lecture/Model	87

Strategies Observed in Visits during February–May 2014
*May not equal total observations because more than one strategy may have been recorded during the observation

Figure 7.8. Summary of Strategies Observed for Four-Month Period

The third step in the expedition is to *set goals and priorities* (see Figure 7.1). The ability to set goals is a vital component of educational leadership. It is imperative to understand, however, that it is not the setting of goals alone that has great effect. Instead, goals provide a sense of purpose and shared direction. When goals are developed with colleagues and school leaders, such as leadership team members, the likelihood of sharing and owning the purpose and plan is increased.

Most district-wide goals emanate from the results of strategic planning meetings or meetings for the purpose of setting the direction of the school. Representative groups that have a vested interest in the school and its effectiveness are part of strategic planning or direction-setting meetings. These groups include parents, students, school teachers, leaders, and community members.

Sometimes the results of surveys from one or more of these groups are included along with other data about past and present student performance that is examined during the meetings. The result of the meetings is a report that includes the perceived strengths and improvement areas to be used by the school leaders of the district and the school board for school direction and improvement. In addition to each group expressing and discussing its expectations, recommendations are included, and the relative level of magnitude of each is offered.

The contents of the report include three to five focus areas in the near future for the school district. Rarely is there a strategic plan or direction-setting report that does not have at least one focus area in teaching and learning. Professional development and professional growth plans may emanate from these areas combined with the results of data from supervision and evaluation of teachers by department chairs, team leaders, and school leaders.

What customarily occurs as part of this third step is that the leader and faculty are faced with a list of goals and needs that may appear overwhelming. The ability to prioritize the order of addressing the focus areas must occur. Figure 7.9 presents a model that may be used to assist the leader and the team in selecting and prioritizing goals.

The two lower boxes in Figure 7.9 should be managed by the principal or leader so that time and energy are not diverted from the most vital goals. It is often the role of the principal to assure the team that pressing needs, such as safety-related goals, will receive attention immediately. However, the leadership team will not take on this responsibility because this team's focus is student and teacher improvement. The leadership team should understand that its priorities are the goals in the top right box relating to professional learning and growth.

Next, the goals in the upper right-hand box should be organized, especially if they may be clustered because they are related. The assertion by faculty is often that there are too many initiatives undertaken at the same

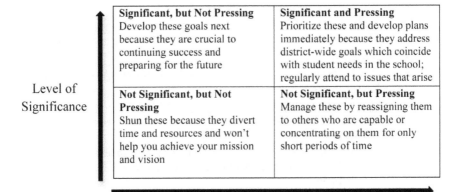

Figure 7.9. **Selecting and Prioritizing Goals**

time. The linkage between and among goals should be expressed as goals are communicated.

Concern and anxiety can be reduced by showing how organizational priorities, which are manifested in the stated district goals and the needs of the building, can be viewed together to address school-wide as well as district-wide priorities simultaneously. The financial resources and available time and expertise are important factors to consider in relation to the goals.

Figure 7.10 illustrates goals developed for one school district. The *values, mission, and vision* of the school are prominently displayed, and the objectives follow. The figure shows how one of the schools in the district, a middle school, worked from the district goals and made them specific and appropriate for their students and individually for teachers.

Values
We can succeed if we work together
Mission
To provide educational excellence in a safe, nurturing environment in every classroom through collaboration among students, teachers, parents, administrators, and the community
To empower passionate, multicultural learners to cultivate their individual strengths and inspire them to be resilient and purposeful community members
Vision
To foster cultural consciousness, challenging each of our students to develop socially, emotionally, and intellectually to their highest potential prepared for high school, college, and career
District-wide Goals based on Mission and Vision
1. Refine instruction to optimize individual student achievement in all curricular areas
2. Embrace the diverse community and increase cultural awareness
3. Demonstrate open communication between all interest groups
Middle School Goals based on District-wide Goals
1a. Develop individual achievement goals with students based on assessments each trimester
1b. Modify and expand instructional strategies based on research based practices in each content area
2a. Emphasize student awareness of and sensitivity to diversity
2b. Increase parent and community involvement in our school of all diverse community groups
3a. Increase communication between school and home about student's progress, behavior , and extra-curricular opportunities in a variety of ways including through technology
3b. Expand communication and outreach to diverse groups in the school using technology

Figure 7.10.   Sample Middle School Goals Based on District-wide Goals

The three major goals developed at the district level were examined by the middle school team. The middle school team noted that one of the district goals was in the area of academic achievement. The second was in the area of cultural awareness and sensitivity. The third was in communication.

The middle school utilized data from its needs assessment, combined it with district priorities based on the *mission* of the schools, and made building goals more specific and applicable to the students, teachers, and families in grades six through eight. Students expressed needs for more opportunities to use technology and to be treated with respect by more of their peers. Needs expressed by the faculty included students taking more responsibility for their learning and parents being more active partners in the school.

Goals 1a and 1b represent the responsibilities for both the student and the teacher. Student goal one includes learning how to set goals based on information regarding students' performance and learning how to express what methods and strategies could assist them in understanding the content or mastering the skills. Teacher goal one includes learning how to have an effective goal-setting conference with students and how to modify or expand teachers' teaching strategies to meet the individual needs of students. The strategies will include using new resources, which will include technology, and both students and teachers will need to access these resources.

Goals 2a and 2b prompt more interaction among parents, community members, teachers, leaders, and students. These interactions promote a greater comfort level to members from diverse cultures entering U.S. school buildings. They provide students with opportunities to interact in a familiar environment with members from diverse backgrounds. The opportunity to expand exposure to more cultures is fostered along with reflections that increase one another's sensitivity to the uniqueness of each group as well as commonalities.

Finally, goals 3a and 3b emphasize communication flow between and among the school and the home and the school with the diverse community. Technology is emphasized due to its power and convenience in sharing information with parents and its ability to facilitate translation of important school events into the diverse languages spoken by parents in the school. Goals 3a and 3b enhance goals 1a, 1b, 2a, and 2b by emphasizing the role of all forms of communication in assisting students in reaching academic goals and greater understanding of diverse cultures.

Prioritizing is again necessary. Which goals will be more costly in terms of time and resources that the district does not presently have? The district reviews the goals with the school board and determines that the technological infrastructure is a resource that needs strengthening.

Researching appropriate software to be utilized is necessary. Purchasing new hardware for use by parents who do not have access along with training them is needed. Selecting and preparing a core of individuals who are recruited to use the new software program and share it with parents is required. Additional budgetary resources are not currently available and will take time to secure over the next three years.

Similarly, the goal to embrace the diversity in the community will include outreach to the various cultural businesses, organizations, and groups. The possibility of partnering with one or more of the cultural businesses, organizations, and groups requires investigation regarding the prior goal of increasing lines of communication, too. The building of these resources and bridges are the responsibility of district leaders including the superintendent, the assistant superintendent for instruction, and the assistant superintendent for business in year one.

Refining and expanding instruction to maximize individual student achievement is assigned as the focus for the schools. In doing so, this goal becomes the responsibility of the principal and faculty members in the school. The two other goals, cultural awareness and communication, are not minimized and may actually be incorporated to some extent when goal 1 is addressed by the teachers individually and as a group. In this way, all three goals are addressed in year one, but the priority for each group and level is clearly stated.

The budgetary resources are considered and new funds for goal 1 are not prohibitive. However, the way in which teachers, department chairs, and the school leaders use their classroom, planning, and meeting times may need to be different than it is at present. In the next step, planning to address goal 1 will take place as part of professional learning and growth.

Finally, building the *capacity* to implement the new strategies should be considered. The questions to be asked include: What is the present knowledge base and skill level of the faculty related to goals 1a and 1b? What gaps exist? What support can be built to facilitate successful implementation?

PLANNING THE ROUTE

The fourth step in the expedition is to *develop a professional learning and growth plan for the school* (see Figure 7.1). The *plan* includes action steps and incorporates *communications, resources,* and *capacity building* of the leaders and the teachers. The *plan* includes the specifying of a time line, the sequencing of actions, and the assigning of individuals who will be responsible to ensure that the professional learning and growth plans are implemented with fidelity. As chapter 3 stated, *professional development* includes *multiple training and development programs that are ongoing and comprehensive.*

The communicating of the goals cannot be overemphasized. As we learned in step one in this expedition, the values, mission, and vision not only need to be developed, but also public sharing and reference to them must be ongoing. Likewise, the goals of the district and the goals at the school level should be connected and frequently discussed.

The plan should make reference to the resources that will be needed and include time to build knowledge, skills, and dispositions of the leaders and teachers. If teachers have partial knowledge and partial skill sets, the school may be able to develop an action plan with a shorter time line. Otherwise, a longer time line may be needed.

The fifth step in the expedition is to *determine the checkpoints and develop process tools* (see Figure 7.1). *Checkpoints* are "stopping places" where the plan will be examined for signs that it is working. *Process tools* are instruments developed to garner feedback or data from individuals and groups by members of the leadership team. Many leaders skip this step or embed it in step four. They wait to see progress at the end of the year or wait to see how the plan unfolds. This may not be the wisest course of action.

This fifth step holds a unique place in the professional learning and growth expedition outlined in this chapter because it is so critical. When the plan is written, the signs the leadership team members will use to verify that the plan is working need to be discussed and specified. The signs might take many forms, but clarity is necessary so all are expecting similar results at crucial points. All need to be moving in the same direction when the expedition begins and as it progresses.

Another critical sign that the plan is working is examining student and teacher performance. Both formal and informal signs should be noted. For example, the percentage of students or teachers able to meet expectations should be posited so every leader can gauge the progress of groups as assigned in relation to goal 1a, developing individual achievement goals.

Figure 7.11 presents the initial stage in the action plan of the middle school with attention to professional learning that illustrates steps four and five of the expedition. The focus in this figure is the preparation of the leadership team and the beginning phases of implementation of the plan throughout the building in year one. This plan focuses on professional learning and growth at the school level.

The principal and leadership team spend the preceding March and April of the coming school year in a neighboring school to observe the skills used by teachers in action with the proper resources. Planning builds from that visit to write a specific plan for the middle school. Protocols and forms are developed as process tools for implementation.

Year 1 Middle School Goals based on District-wide Goals 1a. Develop individual achievement goals with students based on assessments each trimester 1b. Modify and expand instructional strategies based on research based practices in each content area		
Action Plan	**Timeline Responsibility**	**Process Tools and Checkpoints**
1a.1. Leadership team visits neighboring school to meet with teachers who have implemented goal setting meetings with students and observe a class period during which this is done.	March Principal	
1a.2. Leadership team meets to discuss and modify the process as it could be adapted in the school.	April Principal	-Proposal written with timeline -Protocols written
Year 1 August through October		
At the opening of the school year, the superintendent shares the three goals for the district in the next five years in a meeting with faculty from all buildings.	August Superintendent	
Principal shares with the 6–8 building that the leadership team has met and decided to prioritize Goal 1 for the next two years.	August Principal and leadership team	
1a.3. Leadership shares its visit and proposal with the entire faculty; grade level meetings are held to garner feedback.	August Principal and leadership team	-Proposal and Timeline are adjusted -Feedback Facilitation Tool -Feedback is 50% or more in support of the plan
1a.4. Professional development begins with leadership team members modeling a typical goal-setting session with a student and guided practice.	September Principal and leadership team	-Ten minute videos developed -90% of faculty can share -70% can repeat process with a partner
1a.5. Goal setting for the first trimester begins with one class period; class folders are reviewed by the leadership team; 1-1 follow-up meetings are held with each teacher to refine; this is considered a trial run.	October Principal and grade level team leader	-Folders contain one goal for each student -Student goals reflect data used at 80% -Follow-up conducted with faculty as needed

Figure 7.11.   Initial Phase of the Middle School Action Plan

The role of the superintendent, principal, and leadership team at the beginning of year one is an illustration of the communication that must accompany the plan. In August of Figure 7.11, the draft plan is shared with the middle school faculty, clarified, and adjusted. Feedback from teachers is solicited and checked against the 50 percent or more support level expected. Professional learning for the entire faculty begins in September at the department and team levels.

Leaders model a ten-minute goal-setting meeting that has been videotaped with a student during one grade level meeting. The guided practice is staged between two colleagues, with one playing the part of the student a week later, during another meeting. Questions and concerns are discussed and resolved. At one of the checkpoints, the leadership team compares notes to see whether 90 percent of the faculty can explain the process accurately and 70 percent can demonstrate it with a partner. *time of visit*

In October, each teacher will meet with individual students to examine assessment and performance data and set one goal in the teacher's content area. The leaders will observe each teacher at least once for a ten-minute goal-setting meeting. The goals can be from content areas across the middle school curriculum.

The student goals include strength and cardiovascular goals in fitness and health; performance expectations in art, music, and foreign languages; and targets in language arts, mathematics, social studies, and science. Feedback is provided at the end of the month regarding this first goal-setting effort. Leaders examine student goal sheets and record the percentage that used data correctly to form a goal.

In January, as the second trimester begins, the leadership team prepares the faculty for the second round of goal setting with students. Figure 7.12 illustrates the middle phase of action steps, checkpoints, and process tools. During two, forty-minute professional development sessions, emphasis is placed on the use of data from the January assessment in relation to the October assessment. A quick chart is to be drawn by each student to visualize progress. Then the teacher and student decide whether to continue the goal or write a new one. Student goals are checked by leaders, and walk-throughs are conducted.

In January, also, as the teacher and student discuss progress toward the goal, the student shares what the teacher has done that has helped him or her learn and what might be of assistance in the next two months. After goal setting occurs for the entire class, the teacher synthesizes what changes in teaching strategy could be made and sets a personal goal to develop that strategy. Teachers form partners or groups using a shared Google document as they learn and build skills together in February. Leaders monitor the Google doc and confer with teachers as needed.

Year 1 Middle School Goals based on District-wide Goals 1a. Develop individual achievement goals with students based on assessments each trimester 1b. Modify and expand instructional strategies based on research based practices in each content area		
Year 1 January through February	Timeline Responsibility	Process Tools and Checkpoints
1a.6. Goal setting for the second trimester begins; student reviews progress in first trimester goal with teacher and sets goal for second trimester; class folders are reviewed by the leadership team; 1-1 follow-up meetings are held with each teacher.	January Principal and grade level team leader	-Class folder contains one goal for each student using the correct form -Student goals reflect data used at 80 percent -Follow-up conducted with faculty as needed -Walk-through tool to confirm goal setting
1b.1. Teacher selects one instructional strategy to modify/expand during trimester 2 and 3 based on performance of students; new teachers participate in initial years coaching and mentoring program instead.	January Principal	-Strategy either mirrors what individual professional learning and growth plan targeted or selects a new strategy for growth
1b.2. Google doc is created so teachers may share the instructional strategy to be targeted during semesters 2 and 3; each teacher selects one or more colleagues with whom to partner.	January Principal	-Principal reviews Google doc to ensure that each teacher has selected a strategy and at least one partner with whom to work
1b.3. Teachers read professionally and meet with grade team leader or administrator to explain how the strategy chosen will help more students succeed, and what support and resources are necessary.	February Principal and grade level team	-Strategy/Resource Tool -Review of resources are matched to strategy goals

Figure 7.12. Middle Phase of the Middle School Action Plan

Figure 7.13 illustrates the action steps, checkpoints, and process tools in the final phase of the year. In March, the third round of goal setting takes place with the student. By this time, the process should be familiar to teachers and students. The student shows progress by adding to the prior chart or creating a new one. This time, more focus is placed on the discussion with the student of how he or she best learns. The strategies the teacher has added or adjusted are emphasized during the ten-minute session.

The teacher uses this information as part of continuing, formative assessment regarding his or her personal goal to use a new strategy or adjust a prior one. Partners continue to meet to share what is working as they try new strategies. The department chair and leadership team conduct informal walk-throughs in March to note successes and challenges and share progress. Students record their progress for the final time on their personal charts at the end of May. Leaders monitor student charts and visitation schedules.

As the year closes, the students, teachers, and leadership team reflect on their growth in the areas of personal goals and school goals. Short, written statements are especially effective for students to capture the progress over the whole year and share with parents and friends. Teachers and leaders verbalize their journey, while the leader takes responsibility to quantify progress using individual and group data.

When distinctive, new knowledge and skills are necessary, a different plan might be developed than the one seen in Figures 7.11–7.13. Instead, the leadership team could research strategies or pilot efforts as a small group over an entire year. Then, in the second year, professional development would be launched across the building.

By experiencing the challenges of building new skills, the pilot group can develop solutions to frequently faced challenges. The members can experiment with different options and discover which ones are most effective. Moreover, they find the most tenable solutions that can later be offered to the faculty. This capacity building might take up to one year before professional development is extended to the entire faculty.

The foundation for meeting goal 1b has been provided in year one by having each veteran teacher read best practices and partner with a colleague to modify or expand present practice. The teachers have had the opportunity to take risks in trying new strategies without the onus of individual evaluation. In year two, measurement of the degree to which each teacher can achieve goal 1b or modify or expand a strategy based on one or more student needs will be the focus of his or her *individual professional learning and growth plan* developed with an administrator.

With the values, mission, and vision clear, the capacity of the school assessed and built, the goals and plan developed and shared, and the

Year 1
Middle School Goals based on District-wide Goals
1a. Develop individual achievement goals with students based on assessments each trimester
1b. Modify and expand instructional strategies based on research-based practices in each content area

Year 1 March through June	Time Line Responsibility	Process Tools and Checkpoints
1a.7. Goal setting for the third trimester begins; student reviews progress in first and second trimester; sets goal for third trimester; class folders are reviewed by the leadership team; 1-1 follow-up meetings are held with each teacher to share teaching progress; walk-through is conducted by leadership team.	March Principal and grade level team leader	-Class folder contains updated goal for each student -100 percent of the students have charted progress - 1-1 meetings reported in the aggregate reflect 80 percent or more are working toward a teaching strategy to improve student learning -Walk-through data are within 10 percent of verbal reports of teachers
1b.4. Plans are developed to use the strategy; released time is provided to visit classrooms of the partner; coach/chair models.	March and April Grade level team leader	-Visitation Schedule -Strategy Observation Tool
1b.5. Teacher reflection occurs with partner and grade level team leader; summative performance of students is reviewed; students record their individual progress on their chart and reflect.	May Grade level team leader	-Visitation Schedule -Strategy Observation Tool
Principal and leadership team reflect on individual progress made by each teacher; notes are made which will be used in individual professional learning and growth plan of the teacher for the next school year.	June Principal and grade level team leader	-Chart Status of Each Faculty Member Regarding Strategy -Note Program Modifications for Year 2

Figure 7.13. Final Phase of the Middle School Action Plan

checkpoints established, the middle school is ready to carry out the plan. Each leader has roles and responsibilities assigned. It is time for the entire school to embark on the expedition.

TRAVERSING THE TRAIL

The sixth step is to *implement the professional learning and growth plan* (see Figure 7.1). Implementation is a team effort and cannot be accomplished by the leader or leadership team acting alone. Successful implementation requires collaboration. It requires a change in thought, action, or attitude. Sometimes it includes a combination of two or all three of these changes. It is fostered by a school culture in which trust and persistence are valued. It is facilitated by communication that is frequent and affirming.

School improvement requires a concerted effort on the part of a school's members that leads to positive results. The teachers and leaders should feel collective responsibility for the outcomes of the students. Positive results are obtained not only due to agreement on the mission of the school but also to the effect that joint efforts by leaders and faculty have on students.

Possible impediments to professional growth and learning should be examined and removed by the leader. Is the school organized so the plan can be implemented? Has the human side of the effort been part of the equation? What about the political forces that mandate or impede direction? Do our traditions and visual reminders enhance the reaching of our goals or hamper them?

Using the middle school implementation plan as illustration, the leaders responded to the concerns expressed by the faculty during implementation that they needed more release time with their team either during school or additional allocated time after school. The leaders provided choice to each team regarding the best structure that would meet both their professional needs and personal lives outside school hours. Most teams met during school hours, but partners working on strategies together had the flexibility to meet before or after school for additional compensation.

Similarly, human resource considerations revealed that some feared making changes, while others wanted to add new strategies but needed support to learn the new skills. Fear is a powerful force that immobilizes a person from action, while support encourages the individual to make additional attempts at mastery. Leaders assured teachers that any new strategies attempted would not be part of the individual evaluation of a teacher in the first year. All efforts, however, included the fostering of social support to encourage partners to seek and try solutions together.

Political pressures from parents were minimized for the teacher by having the administration explain during open house gatherings and in newsletters that middle school students were learning how to set personal goals during the year. They would have three opportunities to practice taking on this responsibility this year before it became part of the grading rubric in the following school year. Student portfolios included the visible charting of the selected goal and monitoring progress toward it, which served as a symbol that the responsibility to learn and grow requires student as well as teacher commitment.

Some researchers recommend that change is facilitated by encouraging people to change their routine actions quickly as long as support is present. "Just try it," is a common form of encouragement. If success is found, rapid changes in thought and beliefs about the strategy and student will occur. However, people are different. Some are more methodical and must consider the benefits, drawbacks, and consequences before changing an action. Caution is preferred. Change in smaller increments may follow.

Still others, including Fullan and Langworthy (2014) are beginning to write about the kinds of *learning tasks* that teachers assign to students and, by extension, the kinds of tasks that teachers are asked to undertake. The discussion of creating tasks accompanies the debate about the root of implementing the *Common Core State Standards* and new teacher evaluation systems in many school districts. Is moving from a set of state standards to a set of national standards with higher expectations really enough or better than before to ensure school improvement?

Developing *deep learning tasks,* those that involve changing the learning process of students, is really part of the standards reform movement. To change the learning process for students, it is an imperative that the teacher be cognizant of what processes the students will be expected to use. This shift may be accompanied by the development of new strategies for the teacher, which becomes a *deep learning task* for the teacher that can be assisted by professional learning and growth.

As the student shifts from passivity in taking notes from one reliable source, a teacher, to finding credible information from reliable sources on the Internet, a *deep learning task* has been developed for the student. Simultaneously, a *deep learning task* may have been developed for the teacher as well. Instructional preparation shifts from preparing a lecture to how to find, organize, and evaluate credible resources on the web. If the teacher is not comfortable with technological resources and technology, the learning task becomes deep for the teacher, too.

Drawing from chapter 4 of this book, professional learning and growth flourishes when the culture of the building embodies respect and trust. Are multiple perspectives invited and debated as part of solving problems? Do faculty members abandon hope or keep trying? What are reactions by colleagues and leaders when attempts are made? Can teachers share their innermost feelings as they learn? The support system addresses these questions and concerns.

The establishment and ongoing role of *professional learning communities, PLCs,* is an important support system discussed in prior chapters. Mentors and coaches provide feedback, facilitate groups, and locate resources as part of the support system. Teacher leaders and department chairs often add important content expertise to the support. Principals and other school leaders lend support by ensuring that the expertise and resources needed are available and providing various forms of incentives including recognition of the contributions made to the success of the implementation.

Common to all these support systems is the significant role that communication plays. Tomal, Schilling, and Wilhite (2014) discuss how interpersonal communication, including verbal and non-verbal messages, can be improved by attending to the needs of teachers engaged in professional learning and growth. Good communication begins with effective listening. Figure 7.14 provides one model for *effective listening.*

Building on this paradigm is providing *effective feedback.* Chappuis (2012) shares five characteristics of effective feedback between teacher

---

Begin by understanding the perspective of the faculty member and his or her needs rather than that of your own or that of the school

⬇

Restate the main points of the faculty member in your own words so you make certain that you have heard and understood the relevant messages

⬇

Use non-verbal responses including body language to indicate you are listening

⬇

Share empathy with the person and perspective as a colleague

Figure 7.14.   An Effective Learning Paradigm

and student. Three of them relate to the broader principles of when to provide feedback, where to place the focus, and what the feedback should accomplish. Added to these principles should be two more principles, how to offer it and what to do when a stalemate is evident.

Feedback should be provided while the teacher is learning the new content or skills rather than at the end of the year. The focus should be placed on the accurate parts of the partial understandings that the teacher has mastered rather than the errors. The feedback should lead the faculty member to discover the error rather than telling him or her the shortcoming. The feedback should be offered using "we" messages rather than "you" messages that reflect the *school culture* that learning is pursued together. Finally, a compromise should be available rather than a stalemate when no resolutions are evident.

The seventh step is to *monitor the professional learning and growth plan and make decisions* (see Figure 7.1). The monitoring step should be less onerous because of the creation of the checkpoints and process tools in step five. The leadership team should be guided by the time line and level of expectations. An electronic dashboard was created on the school server so that checkpoints could be reported as completed. This encouraged the leaders and teachers to work collaboratively toward the goals.

The leadership team found that the teachers and students met or exceeded the expectations for goal setting by students, goal 1a, in October, January, and March and confirmed their conclusions by examining the student portfolios and comparing notes from the walk-throughs. At the end of the year in May, student portfolios were completed only at the 60 percent level. Teacher feedback revealed that the final goal meetings were begun too late in the year, so the plan for the next school year was adjusted to ensure adequate time was available.

The leadership team and principal monitored goal 1b, the modification or expansion of an individual strategy, and found that the selection and partnering of faculty took place but that classroom visits to one another's room occurred at only a 50 percent rate. Those who visited and shared feedback found the sessions useful as reported on the observation process tool. A short survey was added to the plan in June asking teachers to rate their perceptions of the value of the visit by colleagues and to suggest ways to improve the process.

Surprising to the leadership team was a number of logistical suggestions that would improve the facilitation of the visits. Few teachers who indicated they had not made visits were opposed to the concept but found leaving their classes problematic. The leadership team adjusted plans for the upcoming year to provide two compensated sessions during the school day when a teacher could use personal planning time, not *PLC* or team time, to make a visit to a partner's room.

It was discovered, also, that the tightening of the relationship between the individual learning and growth goal for professional development and school goal 1b would be necessary in year two. Teachers hoped that the two would become more closely linked or actually be the same goal. The principal concluded that this could be done in the majority of the cases.

The main decisions are whether to continue the present course, make adjustments to the plan, or abandon the plan entirely. This middle school did not decide to abandon a part of the plan or the entire plan, but it is valuable to consider this option. Some school leaders would state that they would never choose this course of action; however, it is a viable one when the plan is not showing signs of effectiveness.

The absence or loss of resources could cause a school or district to decide to abandon a plan. The finding that professional development was inadequate to build capacity would be another example, and a new plan might be necessary. When a plan is abandoned, it should be done with care and communication that explains the reasons with openness and honesty to build the bond of trust between faculty and the administration.

REFLECTING ON THE JOURNEY

The eighth, and final step, is to *reflect on the expedition and celebrate the accomplishments* (see Figure 7.1). Sometimes there is a feeling of relief that the journey has finally ended. Other times, there are feelings of exhaustion and questioning whether the efforts were truly worthwhile or made a difference. It is imperative that the data collected, both formal and informal, be given consideration at this time.

Close examination may result in concentrating too much on what was not accomplished or what is yet to be done. The leader needs to take charge at this point. With the same care taken in steps five and seven, developing checkpoints and monitoring them, the results of the journey begin with an objective report of the formal signs of improvement in student learning.

Analysis of data in the aggregate by school and disaggregated data by group, classroom, and individual level should be made. Every indicator of success calls for celebration at the team, department, or school level. Accompanying this type of data should be results reported from the meetings, observations, and other graphic indicators.

Next, an examination of the professional learning and growth of the teachers and leaders should be celebrated. This should be done in relation to both student growth and personal growth. Teachers were asked to record progress and use student portfolios as evidence. Attached to this record would be their personal reflection of growth in the strategy they selected with a note from their partner. The middle school leaders created certificates of accomplishment, both heartfelt and humorous, to commemorate progress toward the school goals.

There was agreement that some of the procedures could be streamlined and that the availability of more technology could speed up and enhance the work of next year. The middle school would focus on goal 1b in year two, but the accomplishments at the district level regarding diversity and communications would begin to have an effect at the middle school level.

The principal and leaders compiled evidence of milestones in the work of the middle school teachers in goal setting with students and strategy development. The middle school leadership team captured candid photos and recorded videos with the consent of individual faculty members throughout the year. This form of concrete illustration helped all to reflect on what had been undertaken and achieved. The school concluded that the journey, though arduous, had been worthwhile. The summer ahead would provide time for renewal and reflection so that all could be ready for next year.

SUMMARY

A professional learning and growth expedition is a journey worth taking for teachers and leaders when members are focused on school improvement and continual, professional evolution. This final chapter charted a course for a leader who is charged with and committed to building the capacity of teachers and leaders to be effective and successful on their journey. Supervising, evaluating, and developing teachers is necessary.

The expedition began with the examination of the values, mission, and vision of the district and school. Laser-like focus on the values, mission, and vision provided a compass when decisions had to be made regarding student and teacher growth. Assessment of the present capacity of the faculty must be included when planning for professional development. Goal setting assisted in prioritizing important targets to guide the journey and keep the expedition focused on its purpose.

The expedition might have been undertaken by one individual, but the outcome would have been very uncertain. The leader selected members to form a leadership team and collaboratively planned the specific actions to promote professional learning and growth. The actions included the development of a time line with responsibilities, the procurement of resources, and the selection of checkpoints and process tools to assist leaders and teachers in ascertaining whether progress was being made.

When it was time for the journey to begin, all was ready. The leaders and leadership team worked together to ensure that support was available and offered at the right time. Challenges were faced by making adjustments to the plan and modifying the route, but the mission and vision remained uppermost in the minds of all travelers. Teachers followed through by setting goals with students, charting progress, and making adaptations in their own teaching.

When the journey was over, the school members reflected and celebrated. They noted what went well so they could use their learnings in the next journey and revised their thinking and actions to improve the areas that needed attention. Finally, as a group, they celebrated their accomplishments. Next year, they would embark on another journey, but their ongoing, continual, embedded professional growth would help sustain them!

CASE STUDY

New Principal at Apollo School

You have been appointed as a principal of Apollo School in a K–12 district with six K–5 schools, two middle schools, and one high school. You are in a K–5 building that has experienced a high turnover in leadership with three new principals and three new assistant principals in the past five years. Enrollment has been stable in the 450- to 500-student range.

The leadership change has been accompanied by a demographic shift in your school with an increase from 15 percent to 20 percent ELL students in the past five years. The percentage of students from low-income families, receiving Free or Reduced Lunch, has increased from 40 percent to 50 percent. The school climate survey from teachers revealed high scores in feeling safe in the building and the ability to work together. Low scores were in the areas of being consulted before changes are made and lack of consistency in following student handbook policies.

The published values, mission, and vision statement of the district is contained in the following textbox:

Values, Mission, and Vision Statement of Apollo School

Values
We believe that children should be stimulated, challenged, and supported.

Mission
The purpose of Apollo School is to build judgment, knowledge, responsibility, and empathy by engaging the heads, hands, and hearts of all its students. The school offers a stimulating curriculum to achieve intellectually, athletically, and artistically. The school maintains a respectful, positive, and safe environment. The school welcomes parents as partners in education.

Vision
The school wishes to stimulate curiosity, foster a love of learning, and develop the ability of students to take appropriate risks to attempt new undertakings.

Test scores have declined in the past five years from 75 percent meeting and exceeding state standards to 65 percent meeting and exceeding state standards. The declines have been equal in reading and mathematics. Your staff members comprise eighteen classroom teachers; two ELL teachers; three special education teachers; three art, music, and physical education teachers; and a shared speech therapist, social worker, and school psychologist.

You sent a communication to all teachers in June inviting them to make an appointment or visit you during the summer to meet you and share thoughts about strengths and challenges of the school. You invited support staff members, too. About 60 percent of the teachers and support staff visited, and you have started learning about them personally and professionally.

Most staff members shared their contributions to the school in the past years and stated that the change in demographics was the cause for the downturn in schools. Specifically, they said that more low-income and ELL students means lower test scores and the community and school board need to accept this fact.

The superintendent recently published the results of a parent survey from the prior school year. The focus of the survey was what programs should be offered after school and in the summer to increase participation in school-sponsored activities. With a response rate of 70 percent including some ELL parents, responses were evenly split between academic offerings in reading and mathematics and additions of dance and pottery making in the fine arts.

District-level professional development was offered last year to implement the new reading program. Every teacher, except those in art, music, and physical education, attended for six half-days from prior to the end of last year. The consultant presented information and answered questions on six topics (getting started, large and small grouping, using materials, higher-level questioning, assessment, reading and writing connection).

At the building level, some individuals and teams of teachers requested funds to attend conferences. Some shared their learnings when they returned to school, and some did not. A review of annual teacher evaluations revealed 10 percent with a *superior* rating, 70 percent with a *proficient* rating, and 20 percent with a *needs improvement* rating.

EXERCISES AND DISCUSSION QUESTIONS

1. How will the values, mission, and vision guide your decisions and priorities?
2. What additional data would you collect and review in your capacity as principal or ask your leadership team to collect and review?
3. Develop goals for your first six months as the new principal of Apollo School in the order of priority. Explain your prioritization.
4. Describe the process you would follow to plan for professional learning and growth as part of professional development in your building for year two.

REFERENCES

Chappuis, J. (2012). How am I doing? *Educational Leadership, 70*(1), 36–41.

DuFour, R. (2014). Harnessing the power of PLCS. *Educational Leadership, 71*(8), 30–35.

Fullan, M., & Langworthy, M. (2014). *A rich seam: How new pedagogies find deep learning.* Retrieved from http://www.michaelfullan.ca/wp-content/uploads/2014/01/3897.Rich_Seam_web.pdf

National Center for Safe Supportive Learning Environments. (2014). *A school climate survey compendia.* Retrieved from http://safesupportivelearning.ed.gov/topic-research/school-climate-measurement/school-climate-survey-compendium

Tomal, D., Schilling, C., & Wilhite, R. (2014). *The teacher leader.* Lanham, MD: Rowman & Littlefield Education, Inc.

Appendix A

InTASC Model Core Teaching Standards

Standard 1: Learner Development—The teacher understands how learners grow and develop, recognizing that patterns of learning and development vary individually within and across the cognitive, linguistic, social, emotional, and physical areas, and designs and implements developmentally appropriate and challenging learning experiences.

Standard 2: Learning Differences—The teacher uses understanding of individual differences and diverse cultures and communities to ensure inclusive learning environments that enable each learner to meet high standards.

Standard 3: Learning Environments—The teacher works with others to create environments that support individual and collaborative learning and that encourage positive social interaction, active engagement in learning, and self-motivation.

Standard 4: Content Knowledge—The teacher understands the central concepts, tools of inquiry, and structures of the discipline(s) he or she teaches and creates learning experiences that make these aspects of the discipline accessible and meaningful for learners to assure mastery of the content.

Standard 5: Application of Content—The teacher understands how to connect concepts and use differing perspectives to engage learners in critical thinking, creativity, and collaborative problem solving related to authentic local and global issues.

Standard 6: Assessment—The teacher understands and uses multiple methods of assessment to engage learners in their own growth, to monitor learner progress, and to guide the teacher's and learner's decision making.

Standard 7: Planning for Instruction—The teacher plans instruction that supports every student in meeting rigorous learning goals by drawing upon knowledge of content areas, curriculum, cross-disciplinary skills, and pedagogy, as well as knowledge of learners and the community context.

Standard 8: Instructional Strategies—The teacher understands and uses a variety of instructional strategies to encourage learners to develop deep understanding of content areas and their connections, and to build skills to apply knowledge in meaningful ways.

Standard 9: Professional Learning and Ethical Practice—The teacher engages in ongoing professional learning and uses evidence to continually evaluate his or her practice, particularly the effects of his or her choices and actions on others (learners, families, other professionals, and the community), and adapts practice to meet the needs of each learner.

Standard 10: Leadership and Collaboration—The teacher seeks appropriate leadership roles and opportunities to take responsibility for student learning, and to collaborate with learners, families, colleagues, other school professionals, and community members to ensure learner growth and to advance the profession.

Source: Council of Chief State School Officers. (2011, April). Interstate Teacher Assessment and Support Consortium (InTASC) Model Core Teaching Standards: A Resource for State Dialogue.

Appendix B

ISLLC Leadership Standards

Standard 1: An education leader promotes the success of every student by facilitating the development, articulation, implementation, and stewardship of a vision of learning that is shared and supported by all stakeholders.

A. Collaboratively develop and implement a shared vision and mission

B. Collect and use data to identify goals, assess organizational effectiveness, and promote organizational learning

C. Create and implement plans to achieve goals

D. Promote continual and sustainable improvement

E. Monitor and evaluate progress and revise plans

Standard 2: An education leader promotes the success of every student by advocating, nurturing, and sustaining a school culture and instructional program conducive to student learning and staff professional growth.

A. Nurture and sustain a culture of collaboration, trust, learning, and high expectations

B. Create a comprehensive, rigorous, and coherent curricular program

C. Create a personalized and motivating learning environment for students

D. Supervise instruction

E. Develop assessment and accountability systems to monitor student progress

F. Develop the instructional and leadership capacity of staff

G. Maximize time spent on quality instruction

H. Promote the use of the most effective and appropriate technologies to support teaching and learning

I. Monitor and evaluate the effect of the instructional program

Standard 3: An education leader promotes the success of every student by ensuring management of the organization, operation, and resources for a safe, efficient, and effective learning environment.

A. Monitor and evaluate the management and operational systems

B. Obtain, allocate, align, and efficiently utilize human, fiscal, and technological resources

C. Promote and protect the welfare and safety of students and staff

D. Develop the capacity for distributed leadership

E. Ensure teacher and organizational time is focused to support quality instruction and student learning

Standard 4: An education leader promotes the success of every student by collaborating with faculty and community members, responding to diverse community interests and needs, and mobilizing community resources.

A. Collect and analyze data and information pertinent to the educational environment

B. Promote understanding, appreciation, and use of the community's diverse cultural, social, and intellectual resources

C. Build and sustain positive relationships with families and caregivers

D. Build and sustain productive relationships with community partners

Standard 5: An education leader promotes the success of every student by acting with integrity and fairness, and in an ethical manner.

A. Ensure a system of accountability for every student's academic and social success

B. Model principles of self-awareness, reflective practice, transparency, and ethical behavior

C. Safeguard the values of democracy, equity, and diversity

D. Consider and evaluate the potential moral and legal consequences of decision making

E. Promote social justice and ensure that individual student needs inform all aspects of schooling

Standard 6: An education leader promotes the success of every student by understanding, responding to, and influencing the political, social, economic, legal, and cultural context.

A. Advocate for children, families, and caregivers

B. Act to influence local, district, state, and national decisions affecting student learning

C. Assess, analyze, and anticipate emerging trends and initiatives in order to adapt leadership strategies

Source: The ISLLC Standards. Interstate School Leaders Licensure, Consortium of Chief State School Officers, 2011.

Appendix C

ELCC Building- and District-Level Standards

ELCC Standard 1.0: A building-level education leader applies knowledge that promotes the success of every student by collaboratively facilitating the development, articulation, implementation, and stewardship of a shared school vision of learning through the collection and use of data to identify school goals, assess organizational effectiveness, and implement school plans to achieve school goals; promotion of continual and sustainable school improvement; and evaluation of school progress and revision of school plans supported by school-based stakeholders.

1.1: Candidates understand and can collaboratively develop, articulate, implement, and steward a shared vision of learning for a school.

1.2: Candidates understand and can collect and use data to identify school goals, assess organizational effectiveness, and implement plans to achieve school goals.

1.3: Candidates understand and can promote continual and sustainable school improvement.

1.4: Candidates understand and can evaluate school progress and revise school plans supported by school stakeholders.

ELCC Standard 1.0: A district-level education leader applies knowledge that promotes the success of every student by facilitating the development, articulation, implementation, and stewardship of a shared district vision of learning through the collection and use of data to identify district goals, assess organizational effectiveness, and implement district plans to achieve district goals; promotion of continual and sustainable district improvement; and evaluation of district progress and revision of district plans supported by district stakeholders.

1.1: Candidates understand and can collaboratively develop, articulate, implement, and steward a shared district vision of learning for a school district.

1.2: Candidates understand and can collect and use data to identify district goals, assess organizational effectiveness, and implement district plans to achieve district goals.

1.3: Candidates understand and can promote continual and sustainable district improvement.

1.4: Candidates understand and can evaluate district progress and revise district plans supported by district stakeholders.

ELCC Standard 2.0: A building-level education leader applies knowledge that promotes the success of every student by sustaining a school culture and instructional program conducive to student learning through collaboration, trust, and a personalized learning environment with high expectations for students; creating and evaluating a comprehensive, rigorous, and coherent curricular and instructional school program; developing and supervising the instructional and leadership capacity of school staff; and promoting the most effective and appropriate technologies to support teaching and learning within a school environment.

2.1: Candidates understand and can sustain a school culture and instructional program conducive to student learning through collaboration, trust, and a personalized learning environment with high expectations for students.

2.2: Candidates understand and can create and evaluate a comprehensive, rigorous, and coherent curricular and instructional school program.

2.3: Candidates understand and can develop and supervise the instructional and leadership capacity of school staff.

2.4: Candidates understand and can promote the most effective and appropriate technologies to support teaching and learning in a school environment.

ELCC Standard 2.0: A district-level education leader applies knowledge that promotes the success of every student by sustaining a district culture conducive to collaboration, trust, and a personalized learning environment with high expectations for students; creating and evaluating a comprehensive, rigorous, and coherent curricular and instructional district program; developing and supervising the instructional and leadership capacity across the district; and promoting the most effective and appropriate technologies to support teaching and learning within the district.

2.1: Candidates understand and can advocate, nurture, and sustain a district culture and instructional program conducive to student learning through collaboration, trust, and a personalized learning environment with high expectations for students.

2.2: Candidates understand and can create and evaluate a comprehensive, rigorous, and coherent curricular and instructional district program.

2.3: Candidates understand and can develop and supervise the instructional and leadership capacity across the district.

2.4: Candidates understand and can promote the most effective and appropriate district technologies to support teaching and learning within the district.

ELCC Standard 3.0: A building-level education leader applies knowledge that promotes the success of every student by ensuring the management of the school organization, operation, and resources through monitoring and evaluating the school management and operational systems; efficiently using human, fiscal, and technological resources in a school environment; promoting and protecting the welfare and safety of school students and staff; developing school capacity for distributed leadership; and ensuring that teacher and organizational time is focused to support high-quality instruction and student learning.

3.1: Candidates understand and can monitor and evaluate school management and operational systems.

3.2: Candidates understand and can efficiently use human, fiscal, and technological resources to manage school operations.

3.3: Candidates understand and can promote school-based policies and procedures that protect the welfare and safety of students and staff within the school.

3.4: Candidates understand and can develop school capacity for distributed leadership.

3.5: Candidates understand and can ensure teacher and organizational time focuses on supporting high-quality school instruction and student learning.

ELCC Standard 3.0: A district-level education leader applies knowledge that promotes the success of every student by ensuring the management of the district's organization, operation, and resources through monitoring and evaluating district management and operational systems; efficiently using human, fiscal, and technological resources within the district; promoting district-level policies and procedures that protect the welfare and safety of students and staff across the district; developing district capacity for distributed leadership; and ensuring that district time focuses on high-quality instruction and student learning.

3.1: Candidates understand and can monitor and evaluate district management and operational systems.

3.2: Candidates understand and can efficiently use human, fiscal, and technological resources within the district.

3.3: Candidates understand and can promote district-level policies and procedures that protect the welfare and safety of students and staff across the district.

3.4: Candidates understand and can develop district capacity for distributed leadership.

3.5: Candidates understand and can ensure that district time focuses on supporting high-quality school instruction and student learning.

ELCC Standard 4.0: A building-level education leader applies knowledge that promotes the success of every student by collaborating with faculty and community members, responding to diverse community interests and needs, and mobilizing community resources on behalf of the school by collecting and analyzing information pertinent to improvement of the school's educational environment; promoting an understanding, appreciation, and use of the diverse cultural, social, and intellectual resources within the school community; building and sustaining positive school relationships with families and caregivers; and cultivating productive school relationships with community partners.

4.1: Candidates understand and can collaborate with faculty and community members by collecting and analyzing information pertinent to the improvement of the school's educational environment.

4.2: Candidates understand and can mobilize community resources by promoting an understanding, appreciation, and use of diverse cultural, social, and intellectual resources within the school community.

4.3: Candidates understand and can respond to community interests and needs by building and sustaining positive school relationships with families and caregivers.

4.4: Candidates understand and can respond to community interests and needs by building and sustaining productive school relationships with community partners.

ELCC Standard 4.0: A district-level education leader applies knowledge that promotes the success of every student by collaborating with faculty and community members, responding to diverse community interests and needs, and mobilizing community resources for the district by collecting and analyzing information pertinent to improvement of the district's educational environment; promoting an understanding, appreciation, and use of the community's diverse cultural, social, and intellectual resources throughout the district; building and sustaining positive district relationships with families and caregivers; and cultivating productive district relationships with community partners.

4.1: Candidates understand and can collaborate with faculty and community members by collecting and analyzing information pertinent to the improvement of the district's educational environment.

4.2: Candidates understand and can mobilize community resources by promoting understanding, appreciation, and use of the community's diverse cultural, social, and intellectual resources throughout the district.

4.3: Candidates understand and can respond to community interests and needs by building and sustaining positive district relationships with families and caregivers.

4.4: Candidates understand and can respond to community interests and needs by building and sustaining productive district relationships with community partners.

ELCC Standard 5.0: A building-level education leader applies knowledge that promotes the success of every student by acting with integrity, fairness, and in an ethical manner to ensure a school system of accountability for every student's academic and social success by modeling school principles of self-awareness, reflective practice, transparency, and ethical behavior as related to their roles within the school; safeguarding the values of democracy, equity, and diversity within the school; evaluating the potential moral and legal consequences of decision making in the school; and promoting social justice within the school to ensure that individual student needs inform all aspects of schooling.

5.1: Candidates understand and can act with integrity and fairness to ensure a school system of accountability for every student's academic and social success.

5.2: Candidates understand and can model principles of self-awareness, reflective practice, transparency, and ethical behavior as related to their roles within the school.

5.3: Candidates understand and can safeguard the values of democracy, equity, and diversity within the school.

5.4: Candidates understand and can evaluate the potential moral and legal consequences of decision making in the school.

5.5: Candidates understand and can promote social justice within the school to ensure that individual student needs inform all aspects of schooling.

ELCC Standard 5.0: A district-level education leader applies knowledge that promotes the success of every student by acting with integrity and fairness, and in an ethical manner to ensure a district system of accountability for every student's academic and social success by modeling district principles of self-awareness, reflective practice, transparency, and ethical behavior as related to their roles within the district; safeguarding the values of democracy, equity, and diversity within the district; evaluating the potential moral and legal consequences of decision making in the district; and promoting social justice within the district to ensure individual student needs inform all aspects of schooling.

5.1: Candidates understand and can act with integrity and fairness to ensure a district system of accountability for every student's academic and social success.

5.2: Candidates understand and can model principles of self-awareness, reflective practice, transparency, and ethical behavior as related to their roles within the district.

5.3: Candidates understand and can safeguard the values of democracy, equity, and diversity within the district.

5.4: Candidates understand and can evaluate the potential moral and legal consequences of decision making in the district.

5.5: Candidates understand and can promote social justice within the district to ensure individual student needs inform all aspects of schooling.

ELCC Standard 6.0: A building-level education leader applies knowledge that promotes the success of every student by understanding, responding to, and influencing the larger political, social, economic, legal, and cultural context through advocating for school students, families, and caregivers; acting to influence local, district, state, and national decisions affecting student learning in a school environment; and anticipating and assessing emerging trends and initiatives in order to adapt school-based leadership strategies.

6.1: Candidates understand and can advocate for school students, families, and caregivers.

6.2: Candidates understand and can act to influence local, district, state, and national decisions affecting student learning in a school environment.

6.3: Candidates understand and can anticipate and assess emerging trends and initiatives in order to adapt school-based leadership strategies.

ELCC Standard 6.0: A district-level education leader applies knowledge that promotes the success of every student by understanding, responding to, and influencing the larger political, social, economic, legal, and cultural context within the district through advocating for district students, families, and caregivers; acting to influence local, district, state, and national decisions affecting student learning; and anticipating and assessing emerging trends and initiatives in order to adapt district-level leadership strategies.

6.1: Candidates understand and can advocate for district students, families, and caregivers.

6.2: Candidates understand and can act to influence local, district, state, and national decisions affecting student learning in a district environment.

6.3: Candidates understand and can anticipate and assess emerging trends and initiatives in order to adapt district-level leadership strategies.

ELCC Standard 7.0: A building-level education leader applies knowledge that promotes the success of every student through a substantial and sustained educational leadership internship experience that has school-based field experiences and clinical internship practice within a school setting and is monitored by a qualified, on-site mentor.

7.1: Substantial Field and Clinical Internship Experience: The program provides significant field experiences and clinical internship practice for candidates within a school environment to synthesize and apply the content knowledge and develop professional skills identified in the other *Educational Leadership Building-Level Program Standards* through authentic, school-based leadership experiences.

7.2: Sustained Internship Experience: Candidates are provided a six-month, concentrated (9–12 hours per week) internship that includes field experiences within a school-based environment.

7.3: Qualified On-Site Mentor: An on-site school mentor who has demonstrated experience as an educational leader within a school and is selected collaboratively by the intern and program faculty with training by the supervising institution.

ELCC Standard 7.0: A district-level education leader applies knowledge that promotes the success of every student in a substantial and sustained educational leadership internship experience that has district-based field experiences and clinical practice within a district setting and is monitored by a qualified, on-site mentor.

7.1: Substantial Experience: The program provides significant field experiences and clinical internship practice for candidates within a district environment to synthesize and apply the content knowledge and develop professional skills identified in the other *Educational Leadership District-Level Program Standards* through authentic, district-based leadership experiences.

7.2: Sustained Experience: Candidates are provided a six-month concentrated (9–12 hours per week) internship that includes field experiences within a district environment.

7.3: Qualified On-site Mentor: An on-site district mentor who has demonstrated successful experience as an educational leader at the district level and is selected collaboratively by the intern and program faculty with training by the supervising institution.

Source: ELCC Standards, November 2011, National Policy Board for Educational Administration (NPBEA), The National Council for Accreditation of Teacher Education (NCATE) now Council for the Accreditation of Educator Preparation (CAEP).

Appendix D

Teacher Leader Model Standards

DOMAIN I

Fostering a Collaborative Culture to Support Educator Development and Student Learning

The teacher leader understands the principles of adult learning and knows how to develop a collaborative culture of collective responsibility in the school. The teacher leader uses this knowledge to promote an environment of collegiality, trust, and respect that focuses on continual improvement in instruction and student learning.

DOMAIN II

Accessing and Using Research to Improve Practice and Student Learning

The teacher leader understands the evolving nature of teaching and learning, the established and emerging technologies, and school community. The teacher leader uses this knowledge to promote, design, and facilitate job-embedded professional learning aligned with school improvement goals.

DOMAIN III

Promoting Professional Learning for Continual Improvement

The teacher leader understands the evolving nature of teaching and learn-ing, established and emerging technologies, and the school community. The teacher leader uses this knowledge to promote, design, and facilitate job-embedded professional learning aligned with school improvement goals.

DOMAIN IV

Facilitating Improvements in Instruction and Student Learning

The teacher leader demonstrates a deep understanding of the teaching and learning processes and uses this knowledge to advance the profes-sional skills of colleagues by being a continual learner and modeling reflective practice based on student results. The teacher leader works col-laboratively with colleagues to ensure instructional practices are aligned to a shared vision, mission, and goals.

DOMAIN V

Promoting the Use of Assessments and Data for School and District Improvement

The teacher leader is knowledgeable about current research on classroom- and school-based data and the design and selection of appropriate forma-tive and summative assessment methods. The teacher leader shares this knowledge and collaborates with colleagues to use assessment and other data to make informed decisions that improve learning for all students and to inform school and district improvement strategies.

DOMAIN VI

Improving Outreach and Collaboration with Families and Community

The teacher leader understands that families, cultures, and communities have a significant effect on educational processes and student learning. The teacher leader works with colleagues to promote ongoing system-atic collaboration with families, community members, business and community leaders, and other stakeholders to improve the educational system and expand opportunities for student learning.

DOMAIN VII

Advocating for Student Learning and the Profession

The teacher leader understands how educational policy is made at the local, state, and national levels as well as the roles of school leaders, boards of education, legislators, and other stakeholders in formulating those policies. The teacher leader uses this knowledge to advocate for student needs and for practices that support effective teaching and increase student learning, and serves as an individual of influence and respect within the school, community, and profession.

Source: The Teacher Leadership Exploratory Consortium, 2010.

Appendix E

Sample Professional Learning and Growth Plans

SUPERINTENDENT

Date: _____

District: _____

Evaluator: _____

Name: _____

Position: Superintendent _____

Performance Rating: _____

Standards: ISLLC: Standards 1 and 2			
Goal: Increase student performance			
Action Steps	*Time*	*Resources*	*Person*	*Evidence*
A. Identify district student performance goals and indicators to measure them for the district, each school, and each student sub-group. 1. Analyze student test data and determine goals for the district, each school, and each student sub-group. 2. Select indicators that will measure student performance in the district, at each school, and for each sub-group. B. Identify research-based instructional strategies. 1. Direct assistant superintendent to identify research-based instructional strategies to be used by all teachers in classrooms. 2. Direct assistant superintendent to develop a professional learning and growth plan for principals and teachers.	August 2014	Allocate budget for stipends to pay district leadership team for work over the summer.	Superintendent and members of board of education	1. Student performance data reported at August board meeting. 2. Student performance learning goals, curriculum plans, and instructional resources presented at August board meeting.

PRINCIPAL

Date: _____
District: _____
School: _____
Performance Rating: _____

Name: _____
Position: Principal
Evaluator: Superintendent

Standards: ISLLC: Standards 1 and 2

Goal: Increase student performance and teacher effectiveness

Action Steps	Time	Resources	Person	Evidence
A. Develop a school leadership team. 1. Select teacher leaders who are representative of school stakeholders to serve on the school leadership team. 2. Examine indicator data to identify school faculty needs for learning and growth. 3. Facilitate preparation of the school professional learning and growth plan for faculty and staff. B. Create organizational processes and procedures that will develop a culture that values continual improvement and lifelong learning. 1. Work with school leadership team to create time during school year for teacher training in team skills. 2. Work with school leadership team to develop collaborative interdisciplinary teams. C. Develop professional learning and growth culture in the school. 1. Coach and mentor teacher leaders. 2. Train teachers in research-based instructional strategies.	August 2014

2014–2015 school year | Allocate funds to pay district school leaders and team members for work over the summer.

Money for release time for school leaders and team to meet, train, and coach and mentor teachers during the school day. | Principal | 1. Student performance data from last school year reported at August board meeting. 2. Student performance goals for new school year presented at August board meeting. 3. School professional learning and growth plan. 4. Interdisciplinary team agendas, minutes, and recommendations for next meeting. |

TEACHER LEADER

Date: _____
District: _____
School: _____
Performance Rating: _____

Name: _____
Position: Teacher Leader
Evaluator: Principal

Standards: ISLLC: Standards 1 and 2

Goal: Increase teacher and student performance

Action Steps	Time	Resources	Person	Evidence
A. Become a member of the school leadership team. 1. Accept invitation to become a member of the school leadership team. 2. Attend meetings and participate in decision making. 3. Conduct action research to improve teacher effectiveness. B. Supervise classroom teachers. 1. Coach and mentor classroom teachers. 2. Conduct formal and informal observations. 3. Provide professional growth training in research-based instructional strategies. 4. Provide professional training in the use of assessments and analysis of data for school and district improvement.	2014–2015 school year	District and school budget allocations to pay school leader team members for analysis of data and development of the school professional learning and growth plan during the summer. District funds for release time to attend meetings and coach, mentor, and train teachers.	Principal teacher	1. Student performance data from last school year reported at August board meeting. 2. Student performance goals presented at August board meeting. 3. Calendar of training sessions and observation of teachers. 4. School professional learning and growth plans.

CLASSROOM TEACHER

Date: _____

District: _____

School: _____

Performance Rating: _____

Name: _____

Position: Teacher

Evaluator: Principal

Standards: InTASC Standards Model Core Teaching Standards

Goal: Increase teacher and student performance

Action Steps	Time	Resources	Person	Evidence
A. Engage student in the learning process so that instruction becomes student centered. 1. Students become cognitively engaged in activities and assignments and content exploration. 2. Students initiate or adapt activities and projects to enhance their understanding. 3. Students take the initiative to influence the formation or adjustment of instructional groups. 4. Students initiate choice, adaptation, or creation of materials to enhance their learning. 5. Pacing of instruction is appropriate for all students. B. Higher order teacher questioning increases student thinking and problem solving. 1. Teacher wait time provides for opportunities for all students to respond to questions and discussions. 2. Students formulate questions.	2014–2015 school year	Money for books and videos that describe distinguished teacher's classroom and student engagement. Money for release time for teacher to observe in a distinguished teacher's classroom. Money for release time for distinguished teacher leader to observe in proficient teacher's classroom in order to coach and mentor.	Principal and Teacher Leader	1. Informal and formal observations with immediate constructive feedback by principal and teacher leader. 2. Proficient teacher observations of distinguished teacher with written report and reflection on each observation. 3. Written summary of collaborative weekly conversations about progress of proficient teacher moving to distinguished performance rating.

Index

About the Authors

Daniel R. Tomal, PhD, Distinguished Professor of Leadership at Concordia University Chicago, River Forest, Illinois. He has been a public high school teacher, administrator, corporate vice president, and professor. He received his BS and MAE degrees in education from Ball State University and a PhD educational administration and supervision from Bowling Green State University. He has consulted for numerous schools and testified before the U.S. Congress, and was voted outstanding teacher at Purdue University North Central. Dan has authored sixteen books and over 200 articles and research studies. He has made guest appearances on numerous radio and television shows such as *CBS This Morning, NBC Cover to Cover, Les Brown, Joan Rivers, Tom Snyder, CBN 700 Club, ABC News,* and *WYLL Chicago Talks.* He is author of the books *Action Research for Educators,* a *Choice* Outstanding Academic Title, *School Resource Management: Optimizing Fiscal, Facilities, and Human Resources* (with Craig Schilling), *Human Resource Management and Collective Bargaining* (with Craig Schilling), and *The Teacher Leader* (with Craig Schilling and Robert Wilhite), all from Rowman & Littlefield.

Robert K. Wilhite, EdD, chair of the Concordia University Chicago's Department of Educational Leadership. He received his BA in Humanities from Southern Illinois University, Masters in Reading and Learning Disabilities, and an EdD in Curriculum, Instruction and Administration from Loyola University Chicago. He is a former elementary, middle school, and high school principal; associate superintendent for curriculum and instruction; and superintendent of schools. He is co-author of *The Teacher Leader* book, from Rowman & Littlefield. He has made numerous presentations at conferences in areas of leadership styles and curriculum development. He also currently serves on the Illinois Licensure Board,

Principal Review Panel, evaluating the design of university principal preparation programs in Illinois.

Barbara J. Phillips, PhD, is currently professor of educational leadership at Concordia University in Chicago. She has been a teacher, a principal, an assistant superintendent for instruction, and director of the School of Education at North Park University in Chicago. She has been the recipient of community, state, and federal grants for teacher and school improvement and regularly serves as a consultant to school districts. She currently teaches courses in school change, data-driven decision making, supervision and evaluation, teacher leadership, and curriculum.

Paul A. Sims is a former teacher and principal in Chicago. He has authored several articles and given numerous presentations on leadership, supervision, and curriculum. He has served as an expert trainer for the new Illinois teacher leader program and has served as a consultant in numerous school districts. He currently teaches in the area of supervision and instruction and is involved in redesigning programs in instruction and curriculum and doctoral school leadership.

Nancy P. Gibson is president of the National ASCD Board of Directors, an international education association. She has traveled extensively with the ASCD and studied educational systems in the countries of Thailand, Cambodia, Argentina, China, Canada, South Vietnam, North Vietnam, Egypt, and most recently Qatar. She is a former elementary, middle school, and high school teacher; principal; assistant superintendent for curriculum and instruction; and superintendent of schools. She is an associate professor at Concordia University Chicago in the leadership department and teaches supervision and improvement of instruction. She recently served as a member of a National Expert Panel for the Apple ConnectEd project.

Lightning Source UK Ltd.
Milton Keynes UK
UKHW021318231122
412709UK00027B/267